THE
Pillsbury
Cook Book

A NEW EDITION

containing more than
Three hundred Recipes
with illustrations and
Menus, selected for their
adaptability to the needs of
the economical American
housewife, with a Popular
Educational Series of over
Seventy Original Drawings,
picturing the Pillsbury
process of Flour Milling
also many other novel
and exclusive features.

TABLE OF WEIGHTS AND MEASURES.

Butter—2 solid cups equal 1 pound.
Butter—2 tablespoonfuls equal 1 ounce.
Butter—4 tablespoonfuls equal 2 ounces or ¼ cup.
Bread—1 cup stale crumbs equals 2 ounces.
Coffee—4 cups equal one pound.
Currants—1 cup cleaned makes 6 ounces.
Cornmeal—1 cup makes 6 ounces.
Dry and solid material—8 tablespoonfuls equal 1 cup.
Eggs—10 shelled equal 1 pound.
Eggs—8 with shells equal 1 pound.
Extract—One-half ounce bottle makes 12 teaspoons.
Flour—4 tablespoonfuls equal 1 ounce.
Flour—4 cups equal 1 pound or 1 quart.
Spice—2 tablespoonfuls ground equal 1 ounce.
Gills—2 equal 1 cup.
Gills—1 wine glass equals one-half gill.
Meat—1 pint chopped equals 1 pound.
Milk—1 pint, or water, equals 1 pound.
Pints—2 (4 cups) equal 1 quart.
Teaspoons—3 make 1 tablespoon.
Saltspoons—4 make 1 teaspoon.
Sugar—2 tablespoonfuls equal 1 ounce.
Sugar—2 cups granulated equal 1 pound.
Sugar—2½ cups powdered equal 1 pound.
Liquid—1 tablespoonful equals one-half ounce.
Liquid—1 cup contains 16 tablespoons.
Liquid—4 teaspoonfuls contain 1 tablespoon.
Raisins—1 cup stemmed equal 6 ounces.
Rice—1 cup makes one-half pound.

All measurements are level unless otherwise stated in the recipe.

TABLE OF PROPORTIONS.

Bread—1 measure of liquid to 3 measures of flour. Batters of all kinds require 1 scant quart of milk to 1 quart of flour.

Flour—1 quart requires 1 pint of butter, or butter and lard mixed for pastry.
    1 quart requires 1 heaping tablespoon of butter for biscuit.
    1 quart requires 1 level teaspoon of salt.
    1 quart requires 3 teaspoons of baking powder.

Gems and Muffins—1 quart of flour requires 1 quart of milk, etc.

Molasses—1 cup requires 1 teaspoon of soda.

Meat—1 teaspoon of salt to 1 pound.

Salt, Pepper, Soda, Spice—1 spoonful is a level spoon. One-half of a spoon is measured by dividing through the middle lengthwise.

Sour Milk—1 teaspoon of soda to 1 pint.

A spoon means that the material should lie as much above the edge of the spoon as the bowl sinks below it. A heaping teaspoon means that the material should be twice as high above the edge of the spoon as the bowl sinks below it. A level teaspoon should hold sixty drops of water. All dry materials are measured after sifting.

A speck is what can be placed within a quarter inch square surface.

2

Selected Recipes

INTRODUCTION.

THREE HUNDRED PRACTICAL RECIPES, compiled by the distinguished authority Mrs. Nellie Duling Gans, who won the Medal of Honor for Perfect Bread at the St. Louis World's Fair, form the main feature of this new edition of the Pillsbury Cook Book. They have been selected more particularly for their value to the busy housewife, who must have substantial, nourishing and attractive dishes at a reasonable cost and effort, than for their demands on mere culinary deftness. This is but a further application of the principle of Selection, which governs in the manufacture of,

PILLSBURY'S BEST FLOUR.

A note-worthy feature of the present book is the series of seventy-five ORIGINAL DRAWINGS presenting the whole Pillsbury process of Flour Milling from the first planting of the wheat until its final appearance as Pillsbury's Best Flour. These drawings, many of them made on the spot, by highly skilled artists, present in an authoritative and attractive manner, the popular aspects of a fundamental, human necessity. The fact that the subject has never been given in such accessible and connected form lends value to this original work.

TIME-TABLE OF COOKING.

Baking.

Bread—(Steamed) brown: 3 hours.
Beans—Soaked and boiled: 3 to 4 hours.
Bread—White loaf: 45 to 60 minutes.
Bread—Graham: 35 to 45 minutes.
Biscuits—Raised: 12 to 20 minutes.
      Baking Powder: 12 to 15 minutes.
Cake—Layer: 15 to 25 minutes.
     Loaf: 40 to 60 minutes.
     Sponge: 45 to 60 minutes.
     Plain: 30 to 40 minutes.
     Fruit: 2 to 3 hours.
Cookies—6 to 10 minutes.
Custard—Baked in cups: 20 to 25 minutes.
Gingerbread—25 to 35 minutes.
Graham Gems—30 minutes.
Pudding—Rice and bread: 45 to 60 minutes.
     Rice and tapioca: 1 hour.
     Indian: 2 to 3 hours.
     Steamed: 1 to 3 hours.
     Steamed plum: 2 to 3 hours.
Pie Crust—About 30 minutes.
Potatoes—1 hour.

Meats: Baked, Roasted and Boiled.

Bacon—Per pound, fried: 15 minutes.
Beef—Sirloin or rib, rare, 5 lb. roast: 1 hour, 5 minutes.
     Sirloin or rib, fried, 5 lb. roast: 1 hour, 40 minutes.
     Rump, rare, 10 lb. roast: 1 hour, 35 minutes.
     Underdone, per lb.: 9 to 10 minutes.
     Fillet of: 20 to 40 minutes.
Simmered, per lb.: Boiled, 20 to 30 minutes.
Chicken—3 to 4 lbs.: 1½ to 2 hours.
Corned Beef—Per lb., boiled: 25 to 30 minutes.
Duck—Domestic: 1 to 1¼ hours.
     Wild: 20 to 30 minutes.
Fish—Thick, 3 to 4 lbs.: 45 to 60 minutes.
     Small: 20 to 30 minutes.
     Long and thin, 6 to 8 lbs.: 1 hour.
Goose—8 lbs.: 3 hours.
Grouse, Pigeons and Other Large Birds—30 minutes.
Lamb Leg—Well done: 1¼ to 2 hours.
Liver—Baked or braised: 1 hour to 1½ hours.
Small Birds—10 to 15 minutes.
Smoked Tongue—4 hours.
Pork—Spare rib, per lb.: 15 to 20 minutes.
     Loin or shoulder, per lb.: 20 to 30 minutes.
Mutton—Leg, per lb.: 10 to 20 minutes.
     Stuffed shoulder: 10 minutes.
Veal—Leg, well done, per lb.: 20 minutes.
     Loin of, plain, per lb.: 15 to 18 minutes.
Ham—12 to 14 lbs., boiled: 4 to 5 hours.
     Piece boiled in cider or water: 15 to 20 minutes.

BOILED.

Summer Vegetables.	Winter Vegetables.
Asparagus—20 to 30 min.	Beans, shelled—1 to 1½ hrs.
Boiled Potatoes—⅓ hr.	Baked Sweet Potatoes—1 hr.
Beets—45 to 60 min.	Boiled Sweet Potatoes—¾ hr.
Cabbage—35 to 60 min.	Boiled Potatoes—1 hr.
Carrots—1 hr.	Beets—3 to 4 hrs.
Corn, green—15 min.	Cabbage—1½ hrs.
Rice, in fast boil. water—20 m.	Carrots—1½ hrs.
Onions—45 to 60 min.	Parsnips—1 hr.
Beans, string—15 to 60 min.	Squash—1 hr.

This applies to young and fresh vegetables.

Time-table for Frying.

Croquettes, Fritters, Doughnuts, Smelts: 3 to 5 minutes.

Time for Broiling.

Chicken—20 to 30 minutes.
Fish—Small and thin: 5 to 8 minutes.
     Thick: 15 to 25 minutes.
Steak—One inch thick: 4 to 6 minutes.
     Two inches thick: 8 to 15 minutes.

Time for Boiling.

Eggs—Soft cooked, not boiling water: 4 to 6 minutes.
     Hard cooked, not boiling water: 35 to 45 minutes.

4

CONTENTS

Recipes.

Three hundred selected recipes, tried and tested, with accompanying illustrations and other valuable information for the housekeeper.

Illustrations.

One hundred sketches descriptive of the cultivation of wheat and the complete process of milling in the manufacture of Pillsbury's Best Flour.

Plowing in early Spring. Harrowing the Fertile Soil. Sowing the Seed of Hard Spring Wheat.

Reapers wending their way through the Golden Fields.

Pillsbury Country Representative.

Shocking the countless sheaves to ripen in the sun. Wheat fields in the Land of "Pillsbury's Best."

The "Wheat Stacks."

The "Traction Engine."

The Wonderful "Threshing Machine." The Country Elevator Along the Railroad.

Weighing the wheat in Hoppers Scales.

Pillsbury's Best
is known everywhere.

6

CONTENTS—Continued.

Recipes.

Page

Illustrations.

The Great Terminal Elevators.

Collecting Samples of Wheat from Cars.

Minneapolis
Chamber of Commerce.

Cash Wheat Dep't.

The "Wheat Pit" and Trading Floor.

Pillsbury's
Wheat Dep't.

State Grain Inspector's Dep't. (Chamber of Commerce.)

Judging the Wheat by its Weight per Bushel.

Miniature Machines used for Milling Samples of Wheat.

Dough Expansion Test.

Pillsbury's
Chemical Laboratory.

Making Ash Determinations.

Cylinder Bake Test for Gluten.

The Accurate Balance Scales.

Receiving the Wheat.

Plowing up the hard packed soil soon after the winter's frost has disappeared

CONTENTS—Continued.

Recipes.

Illustrations.

The harrows cutting up the long furrows plowed in the fertile soil

CONTENTS—Continued.

Sowing the seed of Hard Spring Wheat in long rows of newly harrowed ground

CONTENTS—Continued.

Illustrations.

Pillsbury's Best
is the best.

The "Great Twin Turbine and Rope Drive" that Turns the Wheels of the Pillsbury "A" Mill, the Largest Single Flour Mill in the World.

Packing
Pillsbury's Best.

Filling and Weighing "Pillsbury's Best" in Barrels by Automatic Machines.

Filling and Weighing the Countless Sacks by Automatic Machine.

Small Package Packing Machines.

Chuting the Chutes to Freight Cars.

Loading "Pillsbury's Best" for All Parts of the World.

One of Flour Specials Leaving Minneapolis each Evening.

Delivering "Pillsbury's Best" into the Housewife's hands.

The Pillsbury
Cook Book.

Send a Copy to each of your Friends.

Bread

"He who has no bread has no authority"
"With bread all griefs are less"

BREAD MAKING

GOOD bread is the great need in poor homes, and oftentimes the best appreciated luxury in the homes of the very rich.

Compared with wheat flour, all other bread materials are insignificant.

Of all the important foods, wheat bread contains the most nutrition. Bread made from Pillsbury's Best Flour is richer in good nourishment than any other food article that the world has produced.

HOUSEHOLD WHITE BREAD.

Materials:

1 pint milk.
1 pint water (or 2 pints if milk is left out).
3 quarts (more or less) Pillsbury's Best.
2 cakes compressed yeast.
2 tablespoons sugar.
2 teaspoons salt.
2 tablespoons melted lard (if desired).

Way of Preparing:

To the lukewarm liquid add the yeast, stir until completely dissolved, then add sugar and salt and stir again thoroughly. Add sufficient flour to make a soft batter, stir in the shortening and Beat Well. Now stir in flour until dough is formed sufficiently stiff to be turned from mixing bowl to moulding board in a mass, knead this until it becomes smooth and elastic, adding, if necessary, a little flour from time to time or until it ceases to stick to the hands or moulding board, but be careful not to make it too stiff. Put dough in a greased bowl or crock, cover and set to raise in a warm place, free from draught, for about three hours or until light. When light knead it a second time, place in bowl for another hour or until light, when it may be moulded into loaves, placed in well greased pans and allowed to stand until it has doubled its bulk or more, then bake until properly browned.

BAKING POWDER BISCUITS.

Materials:

2 cups Pillsbury's Best.
2 teaspoonfuls baking powder.
1 teaspoonful salt.
1 cup milk and water (half each).
1 tablespoonful butter.
1 tablespoonful lard.

Way of Preparing:

Sift the flour, salt and baking powder together twice. Cream butter and lard together, and add it to the dry ingredients, using the tips of your fingers. Then add the liquid, mixing with a knife, until you have a very soft dough. Place on your mixing board. Pat out lightly until three-fourths of an inch thick. Cut out and bake in a hot oven for fifteen minutes.

Quantity:

This will make two dozen biscuits.

BAKING POWDER DOUGHNUTS.

Materials:

1 cup sugar.
2 eggs.
2 tablespoonfuls butter.
2 teaspoonfuls baking powder.
2 cups Pillsbury's Best.
1 cup milk.
1 teaspoonful salt.
½ teaspoonful nutmeg.

Way of Preparing:

Cream the butter and sugar, add the eggs, well-beaten, and then the milk.

Sift the flour, salt, baking powder and nutmeg together and add them.

Roll out one-half inch thick, cut out with a doughnut cutter and fry in deep fat.

When they are cool, sprinkle with powdered sugar.

Quantity:

This recipe makes two dozen doughnuts.

BEATEN BISCUITS.

Materials:

1 lb. Pillsbury's Best.
1 teaspoonful salt.
2 oz. lard.
A pinch of soda.
Sweet milk.

Way of Preparing:

Sift the flour, salt and soda. Then work in the lard. Then use enough sweet milk to make a very stiff dough.

The reapers wending their way to and fro through the endless golden fields

Beat for twenty minutes until the dough blisters. Roll out about three-fourths of an inch thick, cut out and prick each biscuit once with a fork, place in biscuit pans, and bake in a moderate oven twenty minutes.

Quantity:
This will make four dozen small biscuits.

EGG BISCUITS.

Materials:

2 cups Pillsbury's Best.	1 tablespoonful butter.
2 teaspoonfuls baking powder.	1 tablespoonful lard.
	1 tablespoonful sugar.
1 teaspoonful salt.	Whites of 2 eggs.
½ cup milk.	

Way of Preparing:

Sift flour, baking powder, salt and sugar together twice. Cream butter and lard together and add it to the dry ingredients, using the tips of your fingers. Then add the milk mixed with the whites of the eggs, mixing with a knife until you have a very soft dough. Place on your molding board. Pat out lightly until three-fourths of an inch thick. Cut out and bake in a hot oven fifteen minutes.

Quantity:
This will make 24 biscuits.

BOSTON BROWN BREAD.

Materials:

2 cups cornmeal.	1 pint hot water.
2 cups entire wheat flour.	1 cup molasses.
	½ cake of yeast.
1 teaspoonful salt.	½ cup lukewarm water.
1 teaspoonful soda.	

Way of Preparing:

Scald the cornmeal with the pint of hot water, then mix in the two cups of entire wheat flour, the molasses and the salt, adding the yeast dissolved in ¼ cup of lukewarm water. Lastly add the soda, also dissolve in ¼ cup of lukewarm water. Pour this batter into greased molds, filling each a little over half, and let them rise until they are nearly full.

Then put the molds into a pot of rapidly boiling water. Boil three hours, take them out and bake them for half an hour.

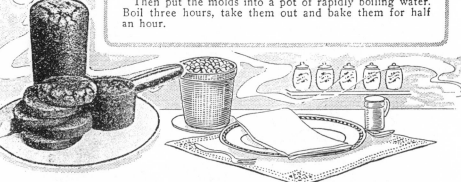

Luncheon
Baked Beans   Brown Bread
Sliced Oranges   Tea

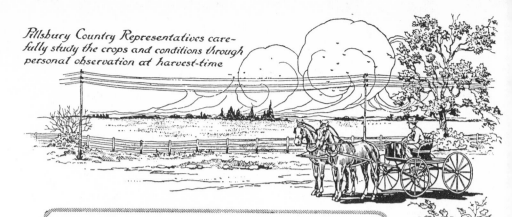

Quantity:
This will make two large loaves.
Note.—In boiling let the water come up to the molds two-thirds of their height, and when it boils away add more boiling water.

SHORT PROCESS FOR BREAD MAKING.

(One of the easiest and best.)

Materials:

1 quart of potato water.
1 dried yeast cake, or ½ compressed, or ¼ cup home made.
¼ cup sugar.

Way of Preparing:

Drain water from potatoes at noon, let cool until luke-warm, add sugar and yeast cake dissolved in ¼ cup warm water, leave this to raise in warm place until next morning, then add 1 tablespoon salt and enough flour (about 3 quarts) to make a dough just stiff enough not to stick to the hands or board; let raise in warm place until 2½ times its size, then put in pans and let raise again 2½ times its size, bake in a moderate oven. May knead dough down once if desired, but not necessary.

CHOCOLATE DOUGHNUTS.

Materials:

2 eggs.	2 tablespoonfuls **melted** chocolate.
1 tablespoonful melted butter.	1 teaspoonful vanilla.
1 cup sweet milk.	3 cups Pillsbury's Best.
¾ cup sugar.	2 teaspoonfuls baking powder.
½ teaspoonful salt.	

Way of Preparing:
Sift together the flour, baking powder and salt. Beat the eggs and add to them the sugar, chocolate, butter and milk. **Then** add the vanilla.

13

Now add the sifted ingredients, making a medium dough. Roll out one-half inch thick, cut out with a doughnut cutter and fry in hot fat. When cool sprinkle with powdered sugar.

Quantity:

This will give three dozen doughnuts.

CORN BREAD.

Materials:

2 cups yellow cornmeal.
2 teaspoonfuls baking powder.
3 eggs.
2 tablespoonfuls melted butter.
2 cups Pillsbury's Best.
1 teaspoonful salt.
1 pint milk.
½ cup boiling water.

Way of Preparing:

Pour the boiling water over the cornmeal, and let it get cool; sift the flour together with the baking powder and salt. Beat the yolks of the eggs until they are light, then add them to the cornmeal and then add the milk, the flour and the melted butter; beat to a smooth batter and beat the whites of the eggs to a stiff froth.

Add the latter to your mixture, stirring it in quickly.

Pour all into a shallow, well-greased pan and bake in a hot oven twenty-five minutes.

Quantity:

Enough to serve six persons.

CORNMEAL MUFFINS.

Materials:

1 cup cornmeal.
1 cup Pillsbury's Best.
1 teaspoonful soda.
1 teaspoonful salt.
¼ cup molasses.
1 cup sour milk.
2 eggs.
2 tablespoonfuls melted butter.

Way of Preparing:

Sift together the cornmeal, flour and salt. Dissolve the soda in the sour milk, and then add it to the sifted ingredients.

Then add the molasses and beat thoroughly. Add the eggs, well-beaten, and lastly the melted butter. Bake in hot, well-greased pans, in a moderately hot oven half an hour.

Quantity:

This will give twelve muffins.

Dinner
Cream of Tomato Soup
Fried Chicken Brown Sauce
Raised Biscuits Suet Pudding
Coffee

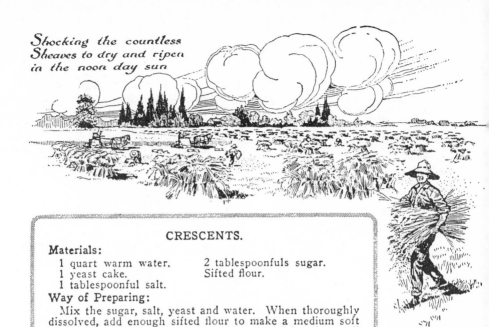

Shocking the countless Sheaves to dry and ripen in the noon day sun

CRESCENTS.

Materials:

1 quart warm water.
1 yeast cake.
1 tablespoonful salt.
2 tablespoonfuls sugar.
Sifted flour.

Way of Preparing:

Mix the sugar, salt, yeast and water. When thoroughly dissolved, add enough sifted flour to make a medium soft dough. Cover, keep in a warm place, and let rise until light, then turn it onto the kneading board. Knead thoroughly and roll out into a sheet one-half an inch thick. Now cut in 6-inch squares, then divide them diagonally, so you will have triangular pieces, brush these lightly with water and roll them up, beginning on the longest side of each. Place into a buttered pan, bringing the two ends around towards each other into crescent shape. Let rise until light, brush with egg and water, and bake. in a moderately hot oven fifteen to twenty minutes.

CINNAMON OR FRUIT ROLLS.

Use same materials and prepare as for baking powder biscuits (page 11).

Way of Preparing:

Roll the sheet of dough into a square. Spread lightly with melted butter. Sprinkle with cinnamon and sugar or with dried fruit. Roll up like a jelly roll, cut off slices about ¾ inch thick and bake.

TWIN BISCUITS.

Use same materials and prepare as for baking powder biscuits (page 11).

Way of Preparing:

Roll the sheet of dough half as thick as for baking powder biscuits. Cut and put two together like a sandwich, with very little melted butter.

EGG BISCUITS.

Use same materials and prepare as for baking powder biscuits (page 11), using 1 egg and less liquid.

BAKING POWDER BISCUITS.

Modifications:

The liquid may be all water or all milk, or half water or half milk. The shortening may be all butter or all lard, or a mixture of both.

15

DOUGHNUTS.

Materials:

2 cups Pillsbury's Best.	1 teaspoonful cream of
½ teaspoonful salt.	tartar.
½ tablespoonful butter.	¾ cup sugar.
½ cup sour milk.	1 egg.
¾ teaspoonful soda.	½ teaspoonful nutmeg.

Way of Preparing:

Sift flour with the salt, sugar, cream of tartar, soda and nutmeg. Beat the egg and add to it the milk. Work the butter into the sifted ingredients and then add the milk and egg. Roll out one-half inch thick, cut out with a doughnut cutter and fry in deep fat.

When cool sprinkle with powdered sugar.

Quantity:

This will make two and one-half dozen doughnuts.

GRAHAM BREAD.

Materials:

4 cups graham flour.	1 heaping teaspoonful salt.
3½ cups Pillsbury's Best.	2 tablespoonfuls brown
2 tablespoonfuls mo-	sugar.
lasses.	½ teaspoonful soda.
3 cups lukewarm milk.	2 tablespoonfuls butter.
1 cake yeast.	½ cup lukewarm water.

Way of Preparing:

Sift together the graham flour, wheat flour, brown sugar and salt, then rub in the butter. Add the molasses with the soda dissolved in it. Next add the lukewarm milk and lastly the yeast dissolved in the lukewarm water.

Knead the dough well for twenty minutes and set it to rise covered up. After rising form it into two loaves, put them into pans and let them rise again.

Graham bread requires longer to rise than white flour bread. Bake in a moderately hot oven for an hour and a quarter.

If graham bread is baked too quickly it is apt to become doughy in the center.

Quantity:

The above makes two loaves of bread.

16

EASY ENTIRE WHEAT BREAD.

Materials:

1 quart entire wheat flour.   ¼ cake yeast.
3 tablespoonfuls sugar.   2 tablespoonfuls **warm**
1 teaspoonful salt.   water.

Way of Preparing:

Sift the flour, sugar and salt. Mix with enough warm water to make a batter, as stiff as it can be stirred. Dissolve the yeast in two tablespoonfuls of warm water, then add it to the batter. Beat for ten minutes. Let rise over night. In the morning beat again. Put in greased pans. Let rise again. Bake in a moderate oven one hour.

Quantity:

This will make one large or two small loaves.

KUGELHUPF.

Materials:

1 cup butter.   1 cup milk.
¾ cup sugar.   4 cups Pillsbury's Best.
7 eggs.   1 teaspoonful salt.
1 cake yeast.   1 cup seeded raisins.
1 teaspoonful vanilla.   2 oz. shredded almonds.

Way of Preparing:

Scald the milk and let it cool. Then make a sponge of the flour, salt and ¾ cup of the milk. Beat ten minutes and add the yeast previously dissolved in the other ¼ cup of the milk. Let stand until light.

Soften the butter, add the sugar and three of the eggs. Then add this mixture to the sponge. Mix thoroughly and add the remaining eggs one at a time. Then add the vanilla and raisins. Butter two Turk's-head molds and sprinkle with shredded almonds.

Half fill them with the mixture and let them stand until they are full. Bake fifty minutes. Turn from molds and cover with powdered sugar.

Quantity:

This makes two loaves.

17

LEMON BUNS.

Materials:

½ cup sugar.	2 eggs.
2 tablespoonfuls butter.	1 cake yeast.
2 cups milk.	½ teaspoonful salt.
1 cup currants.	1 lemon.
¼ cup lukewarm water.	¼ teaspoonful nutmeg.
6 cups Pillsbury's Best.	

Way of Preparing:

Cream the butter and sugar, then add the eggs well beaten. Mix thoroughly and add two cups of flour, then the milk, which must be just lukewarm, then the other four cups of flour. Lastly add the yeast dissolved in the warm water. Beat for fifteen minutes, cover closely and let it rise. When risen, stir in the currants, which must be floured, then add the nutmeg, the grated rind and half the juice of a lemon.

Place on your pastry board, roll out half an inch thick and cut out with a medium-sized biscuit cutter.

Place half the buns in greased biscuit pans, leaving plenty of space.

Then place the other half on top of those already in the pans, making them in pairs. Let rise until very light and bake in a quick oven. After they are done brush the top of each with the white of an egg and sprinkle with powdered sugar.

Quantity:

Three dozen.

LOVERS' KNOTS.

Materials:

1 cup scalded milk.	2 tablespoonfuls melted butter.
2 tablespoonfuls sugar.	
½ teaspoonful salt.	1 egg.
½ yeast cake, dissolved in 4 tablespoonfuls of lukewarm water.	Grated rind of one-half lemon.
	Pillsbury's Best.

Way of Preparing:

Add sugar and salt to the milk. When lukewarm add the dissolved yeast and 1½ cups of flour. Cover and let rise. When light add the well-beaten egg, lemon rind and butter; then enough flour to knead; let rise again. Roll out in a sheet one-half inch thick, cut into strips ½ inch wide and 9 inches long, take up each strip and tie into a knot. Place in a buttered pan, allowing some space between each two, let rise until light and bake in a hot oven from fifteen to eighteen minutes.

MUFFINS No. 1.

Materials:

2 tablespoonfuls butter.	1 pint milk.
2 tablespoonfuls sugar.	2½ cups Pillsbury's Best.
2 eggs.	2 teaspoonfuls baking
½ teaspoonful salt.	powder.

Way of Preparing:

Cream the butter and sugar and add the beaten yolks of the eggs. Sift the flour, baking powder and salt and mix with the former, alternating with the milk. Lastly add the stiffly beaten whites of the eggs.

Have your gem pans hot and well greased, and bake in a hot oven twenty minutes.

Quantity:

This will make eighteen muffins.

MUFFINS No. 2.

Materials:

⅓ cup butter.	1 egg.
¼ cup sugar.	¾ cup milk.
¼ teaspoonful salt.	2 cups sifted flour.
4 teaspoonfuls baking	
powder.	

Way of Preparing:

Cream butter and sugar; add the well-beaten egg. Mix the flour, salt and baking powder and stir in gradually, adding the milk gradually also. Beat thoroughly, turn into hot, greased muffin pans, and bake 25 minutes.

Quantity:

Will make twelve muffins.

NUT BREAD.

Materials:

2 cups milk.	2 tablespoonfuls sugar.
2 cups water.	1 teaspoonful salt.
1 tablespoonful lard.	1 cup chopped nuts.
4 cups Pillsbury's Best.	½ cup lukewarm water.
1 cake yeast.	5 cups whole wheat flour.

Way of Preparing:

Scald milk and water together, and pour them over the sugar, salt and lard. Let cool until medium hot, then add the white flour. Beat ten minutes and then add the yeast, dissolved in the one-half cup lukewarm water. Cover and let rise until very light. Then add the nuts and the whole wheat flour, making a soft sticky dough. Place the dough in a buttered bowl and let it rise until it gains twice its original bulk. Then form into loaves.

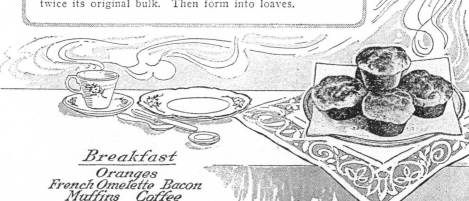

Breakfast

Oranges
French Omelette Bacon
Muffins Coffee

Place them into pans, having each half full, let them rise until the pans are full; then bake them for one hour.

Quantity:

This amount makes three loaves.

PARKER HOUSE ROLLS.

Materials:

3 tablespoonfuls butter.	1 pint milk.
1 teaspoonful salt.	1 tablespoonful sugar.
½ cup lukewarm water.	1 cake yeast.
6 cups sifted flour.	

Way of Preparing:

Scald the milk and pour it over the sugar, salt and butter. Allow it to cool, and when it is lukewarm, add the yeast, dissolved in the lukewarm water, and then add three cups of flour. Beat hard, cover and let rise until it is a frothy mass. Then add three more cups of flour. Let it rise again until it is twice its original bulk, then place it on your kneading board. Knead lightly and then roll it out one-half an inch thick.

Take a biscuit cutter and cut out the rolls. Brush each piece with butter, fold and press the edges together, and place them in a greased pan, one inch apart. Let them rise until very light. Bake in a hot oven fifteen minutes.

Quantity:

This recipe makes three dozen Parker House rolls.

POPOVERS.

Materials:

2 cups Pillsbury's Best.	2 cups milk.
3 eggs.	1 teaspoonful salt.

Way of Preparing:

Beat the eggs until very light. Add the milk and salt and pour gradually into the flour, beating all the time.

Beat the batter very smooth and strain through a sieve. Have your gem pans lightly greased, and very hot. Quickly fill half full of the batter. Place in a hot oven and bake twenty-five minutes. They should feel dry to the touch.

Quantity:

This will make eighteen popovers.

POTATO BREAD.

(See previous pages for bread and potato bread.)

The Traction Engine, a great factor in extensive wheat cultivation and largely depended upon for the power to —

— operate the wonderful Threshing Machines through which whole crops are fed and the grain realized for the market

GRIDDLE CAKES.

Materials:

2 cups Pillsbury's Best.
½ teaspoon salt.
1¾ cups sour milk or but-
ter-milk.

1 teaspoon soda (level).
1 tablespoon melted but-
ter.
1 tablespoon sugar.

Preparation:

Sift the flour, salt and soda together. Add the milk slowly and beat till smooth. Then add the melted butter and fry on a slightly greased hot griddle. If desired, a well-beaten egg may be added at the last, when it will be necessary to use a little more flour. The cakes will be more tender without the egg. These cakes may be made with sweet milk, substituting four (4) level teaspoons of baking powder for the soda. This quantity will serve four or five people.

SWEET POTATO BISCUITS.

Materials:

2 cups Pillsbury's Best.
1 cup buttermilk.
1 tablespoonful sugar.
½ teaspoonful soda.

1 cup mashed sweet potatoes.
1 teaspoonful salt.
1 tablespoonful butter.

Way of Preparing:

Mash the boiled sweet potatoes smooth, add the sugar and then the butter. Dissolve the soda in the buttermilk and add it. Sift flour and salt and add them to the other mixture. Roll out, cut as other biscuits, and bake in a quick oven.

Quantity:

This will make twenty-four biscuits.

NOTES ON BREAD MAKING.

Always use a sponge when dried yeast cakes are used. With home-made or compressed yeast it may be made into a dough at once.

A sponge should always raise at least twice its size, or until it begins to fall.

Dough should always double itself and should increase twice its size when placed in the pans.

Do not let it raise too much in dough, or it will be slow in pans.

Do not have oven too hot, as bread should not brown the first ten minutes, and only gradually after that.

Do not cover when taken out of oven, but allow to cool quickly.

Do not make loaves too large.

Farmers marketing their crop of Hard Spring Wheat at the country elevator

SWEET RUSKS.

Materials:

2 tablespoonfuls sugar.	2 eggs.
2 tablespoonfuls butter.	½ teaspoonful salt.
1 cup milk.	4 cups Pillsbury's Best.
½ cake yeast.	¼ cup warm water.

Way of Preparing:

Cream the butter and sugar, then add the well-beaten yolks of the eggs and then the stiffly beaten whites. Sift in the flour and salt and add the milk gradually. Add the yeast dissolved in the warm water.

Cover and let it rise. When very light, pour it into a buttered biscuit pan, filling it half full. Let it rise until the pan is quite full.

Bake in a moderate oven for thirty minutes. When done cut in long narrow strips.

Quantity:

The above will make rusks for six persons.

TEA ROLLS.

Materials:

2 cups milk.	1 teaspoonful salt.
3 tablespoonfuls butter.	6 cups Pillsbury's Best.
2 eggs.	¼ cup lukewarm water.
1 cake yeast.	1 teaspoonful ground cin-
½ cup sugar.	namon.

Way of Preparing:

Scald the milk, and pour it over the sugar, butter and salt. When it has cooled to lukewarm, beat into it three cups of flour, sifted three times. Then add the yeast, dissolved in the lukewarm water, cover and let it rise until it is a frothy mass. Then add the eggs, well-beaten, the flour and the cinnamon.

Place in a buttered bowl. Let it rise until it has twice its original size. Form it then into small rolls, place them into a buttered pan, and let them rise until very light. Brush the tops with melted butter and bake in a hot oven for fifteen minutes.

Quantity:

This will make four dozen rolls.

COCOA ROLLS.

Cocoa rolls are made by adding to the above one-half a cup of ground cocoa.

VIENNA ROLLS.

Materials:
Same as those used for "Crescents."

Way of Preparing:
The difference in preparing Vienna rolls and Crescents consists in the rolling and shaping.

When the dough is prepared, ready for molding, shape the same as small Vienna loaves about six inches long. Place in a buttered pan, allowing a little space between each two, and let them rise. When light, gash the tops diagonally three times, bake in a moderate oven about twenty-five minutes. If desired you may brush the rolls with beaten eggs and sprinkle with poppy-seeds, in which case you omit gashing them.

WAFFLES.

Materials:

2 cups Pillsbury's Best.	1 tablespoonful melted
1½ cups milk.	butter.
1 tablespoonful sugar.	2 teaspoonfuls baking
½ teaspoonful salt.	powder.
2 eggs.	Honey.

Way of Preparing:
Sift the flour, baking powder, salt and sugar, add the milk and the well-beaten yolks of the eggs. Then add the butter and lastly the stiffly beaten whites of the eggs. Fry on a very hot, well-greased waffle iron and serve immediately with fresh honey, maple syrup, jelly or molasses.

Quantity:
The above will make two dozen waffles.

WHITE CORN BREAD.

Materials:

2 eggs.	1 heaping cup white
½ cup Pillsbury's Best.	cornmeal.
1 cup milk.	2 tablespoonfuls butter.
2 teaspoonfuls baking	1 teaspoonful salt.
powder.	½ cup boiling water.

Way of Preparing:
Beat the eggs without separating whites and yolks, add the milk to the eggs. Sift the flour, salt and baking powder together. Pour the boiling water over the cornmeal and let it cool, then add the flour, salt and baking powder, sifted, and then the milk and eggs. Lastly add the butter, after melting it. Bake in a hot oven for twenty-five minutes.

Quantity:
Sufficient to serve five persons.

Luncheon
Corned Beef Hash   Waffles
Baked Apples   Chocolate

SALT RISING BREAD.

Materials for the Yeast:

1 pint hot water.
1 teaspoonful salt.
1 heaping   tablespoonful
    white cornmeal.

11 heaping tablespoonfuls
    sifted flour.

Materials for the Bread:

10 cups Pillsbury's Best.
1 heaping   tablespoonful
    lard.

1 pint warm milk.
½ teaspoonful salt.

Way of Preparing the Yeast:

Cool the water sufficiently to bear your finger in it,
then add the salt, cornmeal and lastly ten tablespoonfuls
of flour. Beat until smooth, then sprinkle the remaining
tablespoonful of flour over the top of the mixture. Cover
and let stand in a warm place five hours. By that time
the clear water should have risen on top of the mixture.
Drain off this water and beat the mixture thoroughly.
Set aside for another hour, at the end of which time the
mixture should have become light and frothy. It is now
ready for use.

Way of Preparing the Bread:

Sift your flour into your mixing bowl, add the salt,
and with the tips of your fingers work in the lard. Now
make a well in the center of the flour, pour in your yeast
preparation and then the milk. With a spoon begin to
stir and continue until it is too stiff to admit of further
using the spoon. Turn it out on the molding board,
knead until smooth, divide into four parts and place them
in buttered baking pans. having each pan half full. Let
rise until they are full. Bake forty-five minutes.

Quantity:

This will make four loaves in an ordinary sized bread
pan.

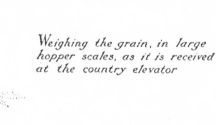

*Weighing the grain, in large
hopper scales, as it is received
at the country elevator*

Cakes

*"Of a good beginning
cometh a good end."*
-- JOHN HEYWOODE

CAKE-MAKING requires more judgment than any other department cf cooking. Nevertheless it is the one most frequently tried by the beginner.

There are two classes of cakes; those with butter and those without it. The former embraces pound, cup and fruit cake. To the latter belong sponge, sunshine and angel cake.

Always mix your cake in an earthen bowl. The baking of cake requires more care than the mixing. Divide your baking time into quarters; during the first it should begin to rise, during the second it should finish rising and begin to brown, in the third it should continue to brown, and during the fourth and last it should finish browning and leave the sides of the pan. Bake your cake with nothing else in the oven and keep it as near the oven center as possible. Remove the cake from the pan as soon as it leaves the oven, and place it on a sieve or a napkin-covered board.

ALMOND TARTS.

Materials:

4 eggs.
1 cup powdered sugar.
½ cup chocolate, grated.
1 teaspoonful baking powder.
½ lb. almonds, blanched and chopped fine.
1 cup cracker dust.
Whipped cream.
Candied fruit.

Way of Preparing:

Beat the yolks of the eggs until very thick, add the sugar gradually, and then the stiffly beaten whites of the eggs. Then add the cracker dust, chocolate, almonds and baking powder. Bake in gem pans. When cold remove the centers and fill with whipped cream. Garnish with candied fruit.

Quantity:

This will make eight tarts.

ANGEL FOOD.

Materials:

1 cup of egg whites, unbeaten.
1¼ cups of sugar.
Pinch of salt.
1 cup sifted Pillsbury's Best.
1 teaspoonful cream of tartar.
1 teaspoonful almond flavoring.

Way of Preparing:

Put a pinch of salt into your egg whites and beat until frothy. Put in the cream of tartar and finish beating. Then beat in the sugar. Add the flavoring and fold in the flour lightly. Bake in an ungreased pan with a tube in a moderate oven for half an hour.

Sift the sugar once, the flour five times, and have the eggs very cold.

Quantity:

This makes one large cake.

CHOCOLATE COOKIES.

Materials:

1 square bitter chocolate.	¼ cup milk.
2 teaspoonfuls baking powder.	2 eggs.
	½ cup butter.
Pinch of salt.	1 cup sugar.
	2½ cups Pillsbury's Best.

Way of Preparing:

Cream the butter and sugar, add the well-beaten eggs, and then the chocolate, melted, sift the flour, salt and baking powder together and add alternating with the milk. Then roll out, cut with small fancy cutter and bake in a moderate oven.

Quantity:

This will make four dozen cookies.

CREAM PUFFS.

Materials:

1 cup Pillsbury's Best.	¼ lb. butter.
¾ cup water.	5 eggs.
Pinch of salt.	Filling.

Way of Preparing:

Heat the water and add the butter and salt; when this mixture boils stir in the flour; take care to have no lumps. Cook until the mixture leaves the sides of the saucepan. Pour out into another pan, and allow it to cool. When nearly cold add the unbeaten eggs, one at a time. Mix in each one thoroughly before adding the next. When all the eggs have been added, cover the mixture and let it stand for one hour. When ready to bake drop it by the spoonful on buttered tins, leaving space for them to rise.

Bake in a moderate oven, for forty-five minutes. They should then feel dry and crisp to the touch. When cold split and fill with whipped cream, custard or jam. If desired, they may be fried in deep fat the same as doughnuts. If you intend frying them drop only teaspoonfuls instead of tablespoonfuls at a time into the fat.

Quantity:

This will make eighteen baked.

DEVIL'S FOOD.

Materials:

¼ cup chocolate.	½ cup butter.
½ cup sugar.	1 egg and 1 yolk.
½ cup milk.	1 cup milk.
1 egg.	1 teaspoonful soda.
2 teaspoonfuls vanilla.	2 cups Pillsbury's Best.
1 cup sugar.	

Way of Preparing:

Put the one-half cup of milk in a double boiler. Melt the chocolate and add to it one-half a cup of sugar, and one egg well beaten. When the milk is boiling hot add it. Put back into the boiler and cook five minutes. Remove and let it cool. Cream together one cup of sugar and half a cup of butter, add one egg and the yolk of another and beat for five minutes. Then add the cup of milk with the soda dissolved in it, and then the flour. Lastly add the vanilla and combine the two mixtures. Mix thoroughly and bake in layers. Put together with chocolate filling.

Quantity:

This makes one medium-sized cake.

LEMON COOKIES.

Materials:

½ cup butter.	2 teaspoonfuls baking
1 cup sugar.	powder.
2 eggs.	3 cups Pillsbury's Best.
2 tablespoonfuls milk.	1 teaspoonful lemon extract.

Way of Preparing:

Cream the butter, add the sugar, the eggs well beaten, milk and lemon. Sift the dry ingredients and add them to the mixture. Chill and roll out thin, using half the dough at a time. Cut in fancy shapes and bake in a moderate oven.

Quantity:

This will make five dozen cookies.

One of the numerous train-loads of wheat on its way to the Pillsbury Mills

LEMON GEMS.

Materials:

½ cup sugar.
2 eggs.
½ cup butter.
Pinch salt.

1 cup Pillsbury's Best.
1 teaspoonful baking powder.
Grated rind and juice of one lemon.

Way of Preparing:

Cream the butter and add the sugar. Add the well-beaten yolks of the eggs and the lemon rind. Sift together the flour, salt and baking powder and add them. Then add the lemon juice and lastly the stiffly-beaten whites of the eggs.

Bake in gem pans in a moderate oven.

Quantity:

This will make eight gems.

LORENA CAKE.

Materials:

1¼ cups sugar.
½ cup butter.
2 eggs.
2 cups Pillsbury's Best.
2 teaspoonfuls baking powder.
1 teaspoonful almond extract.

¾ cup milk.
1 pint whipped cream.
1 square chocolate.
½ cup boiling water.
1 tablespoonful cornstarch.
Grated rind and strained juice of 1 orange.

Way of Preparing:

Beat the eggs and add one cup of sugar, then the butter creamed, one-half cup of milk and the baking powder and flour sifted together, add the grated rind and strained juice of one orange, and bake in a border mold. When cool, but not cold, fill in the center with the whipped cream, piling it up. Then pour around the cake a hot sauce made by cooking one cup of sugar, cornstarch, boiling water, one-fourth cup of milk and chocolate in a double boiler until they have the consistency of thick cream. Flavor with the almond extract. Serve hot.

Quantity:

This will serve eight persons.

NUT COOKIES.

Materials:

⅓ cup butter.
½ cup sugar.
2 eggs.
¾ cup Pillsbury's Best.

1 teaspoonful baking powder.
¾ cup chopped nuts.
1 teaspoonful lemon juice.

Luncheon
Fried Oysters   Deviled Potatoes
Graham Bread   Marble Cake
Milk

The Modern "Terminal Elevator" of fire-proof tile and concrete, where great quantities of wheat are received and stored for future deliveries

Way of Preparing:
Cream the butter and add the sugar and eggs well beaten. Sift the flour and baking powder together. Add the first mixture. Then add nuts and lemon juice. Drop from a teaspoon on an unbuttered baking sheet, leaving an inch space between them. Sprinkle with chopped nuts and bake in a very slow oven.

Quantity:
This will make two dozen cookies.

POUND CAKE.

Materials:

1 lb. butter.	2 tablespoonfuls rosewater.
1 lb. sugar.	½ cup sherry wine.
1 lb. Pillsbury's Best.	
12 eggs, using yolks of nine.	

Way of Preparing:
Cream the butter, gradually adding the sugar, and beat ten minutes. Beat the yolks of 9 eggs until very thick and lemon colored. Then gradually add them to the butter and sugar and beat again. Sift the flour three times and add it slowly, beating all the time. After adding the flour beat for fifteen minutes. Then add the rosewater and sherry and beat again. Lastly, add the stiffly-beaten whites of the eggs. Fold them in, and bake immediately. Use a pan with a tube in the center and bake in a moderate oven for an hour and a half.

Quantity:
This will make one large cake or two medium sized ones.

PLAIN CAKE.

Materials:

½ cup butter.	1 cup raisins.
1 cup sugar.	2½ cups flour.
2 eggs.	1 teaspoonful cinnamon.
1 cup sour milk.	½ teaspoonful cloves.
1 teaspoonful soda.	

Way of Preparing:
Cream butter and sugar; add well-beaten eggs. Dissolve soda in two teaspoonfuls of cold water, and beat it into the sour milk. Combine the mixtures, add spices and flour gradually. Cut raisins and add. Bake forty-five minutes in a slow oven.

Quantity:
This mixtures makes one loaf.

SOFT GINGER BREAD.

Materials:

¾ cup molasses.	3 cups Pillsbury's Best.
1 cup brown sugar.	1 tablespoonful ginger.
½ cup butter.	1 teaspoonful cinnamon.
1 cup sour milk.	1 teaspoonful soda.
3 eggs.	

Way of Preparing:

Cream the butter and sugar, and add the molasses. Then add the eggs, one at a time, and beat thoroughly. Melt the soda in the sour milk, mixing well. Sift the flour and spices and add to the other mixture, alternating with the milk. Bake either in gem pans or in a ginger cake tin.

Quantity:

This will make twenty-four gems or one large cake.

STRAWBERRY SHORTCAKE.

Materials:

4 teaspoonfuls baking powder.	¼ cup butter.
	⅞ cup milk.
½ teaspoonful salt.	2 cups Pillsbury's Best.
2 tablespoonfuls sugar.	Strawberries, 1 quart.

Way of Preparing:

Mix flour, baking powder, salt and sugar and sift twice. Work in butter with fingers. Add milk gradually. Put on board, divide into two parts, and roll out to fit the cake tin; using the least possible flour to roll. Put one part on tin, spread lightly with melted butter, then place other part on top. Bake fifteen minutes in hot oven. When baked, the two parts will separate easily without cutting. Mash berries slightly, sweeten and place between cakes. A dozen or so whole berries may be placed on top for a decoration.

Quantity:

Will cut into eight pieces.

SUCCESS CAKE.

Materials:

2 cups sifted Pillsbury's Best.	3 level teaspoonfuls baking powder.
1½ cups confectioners' XXXX sugar.	1 teaspoonful flavoring extract.
½ cup butter.	½ cup water.
Whites of five eggs.	

Way of Preparing:

Cream the butter and sugar and add the water. Never mind its looks. Then add the flour and baking powder, after sifting them mixed together. Stir this thoroughly and then add the stiffly-beaten whites of the eggs. After that beat it for five minutes. Finally add the flavoring extract, whichever one you prefer and bake immediately.

Quantity:

This will make either a loaf cake or a layer cake.

THREE MINUTE CAKE.

Materials:

2 eggs.
½ cup milk.
1⅓ cups brown sugar.
⅓ cup butter.
1¾ cups Pillsbury's Best.
3 teaspoonfuls baking powder.
½ teaspoonful cinnamon.
½ teaspoonful grated nutmeg.
½ lb. stoned dates, cut in pieces.

Way of Preparing:

Put all the ingredients together in a bowl and beat them for three minutes. Then bake them in a cake-pan for from thirty-five to forty minutes. Be sure to put all ingredients in together; adding them separately will cause failure.

Quantity:

This will make one medium-sized cake.

WHITE FRUIT CAKE.

Materials:

1 lb. Pillsbury's Best.
1 lb. sugar.
Whites of 16 eggs.
¾ lb. butter.
2 teaspoonfuls baking powder.
Rind of one lemon.
1 cocoanut, grated.
1 lb. almonds, blanched and shredded.
1 lb. citron, cut fine.
1 lb. candied lemon peel, minced.
2 tablespoonfuls rosewater.
2 tablespoonfuls sherry wine.

Way of Preparing:

Cream the butter and sugar, add the rosewater and sherry and then the baking powder and flour sifted together.

Beat the whites of the eggs very stiff and fold in. Lastly add the grated cocoanut and other ingredients. Bake for three hours in a slow oven. Use a deep pan with a tube in the center.

Quantity:

This will make one large or two small cakes.

Each car of wheat upon its arrival is carefully sampled by our Experts before it is unloaded

CAKE FILLINGS AND FROSTINGS.

BOILED ICINGS.

Materials:

2 cups sugar.
¼ cup water.

Stiffly beaten whites of two eggs.

Way of Preparing:

Boil the sugar and water until it forms a thick syrup. Then gradually pour it into the beaten eggs, beating the mixture rapidly all the time. When all in, and the mixture has thickened and is cool, it is ready for use in icing cakes.

CARAMEL FILLING.

Materials:

1 lb. brown sugar.
½ cup milk.

2 eggs.
Vanilla.

Way of Preparing:

Boil the sugar and milk until it will harden when dropped into cold water. Beat the yolks of the eggs and the whites separately and then combine them. Gradually pour over them the hot syrup beating all the time. Add the flavoring and beat until cool and quite thick.

CHOCOLATE FILLING.

Materials:

1 cup sugar.
¼ cup Pillsbury's Best.
2 eggs.
2 cups milk.

1 teaspoonful vanilla.
2 squares chocolate.
1 pinch salt.

Way of Preparing:

Heat the milk in a double boiler, mix the dry ingredients and the eggs lightly beaten. Gradually add the hot milk. Return to the boiler and cook fifteen minutes. Melt the chocolate and add it. Cool and flavor.

FONDANT ICINGS.

Materials:

1 lb. sugar.
½ cup water.
XXXX Confectioners' sugar.

1 tablespoonful boiling water.
Flavoring extract.

Luncheon
Macaroni a La Italienne
Parker House Rolls
Chicken Salad
Angel Food with Icing

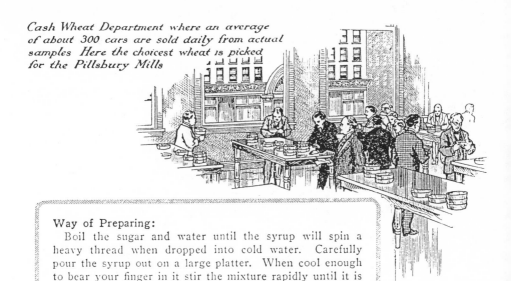

Way of Preparing:

Boil the sugar and water until the syrup will spin a heavy thread when dropped into cold water. Carefully pour the syrup out on a large platter. When cool enough to bear your finger in it stir the mixture rapidly until it is soft, white and creamy. Dust your bread board with XXXX sugar, turn the mixture on it, and knead it as you would biscuit dough, until it is very soft and smooth. Let it cool, place in your double boiler and melt, stirring all the time. Add one tablespoonful of boiling water, flavor to taste and pour over your cake while hot.

MAPLE SUGAR FILLING.

Materials:

½ cup maple sugar,   ½ cup sweet milk.
    grated.   Whites of two eggs.

Way of Preparing:

Put the sugar into an agate saucepan and add the milk. Boil it until it will spin a thread. Have the whites of the eggs beaten very stiff and add the syrup gradually, beating all the time. When it begins to get quite thick place it quickly between the layers of the cake.

ORANGE FILLING.

Materials:

2 oranges.   2 egg yolks.
½ cup water.   ½ lemon.
2 cups sugar.

Way of Preparing:

Grate the yellow rind from the peel of the oranges. Put the water in a saucepan and add the grated orange peel. Boil five minutes and strain. Add enough hot water to make one-half a cup. Now add the water to the two cups of sugar and boil until it spins a thread. Pour it then over the well-beaten yolks of the eggs and beat until cool. Add the juice of half an orange and the juice of the half lemon.

33

Candy

Sweets to the Sweet
HAMLET

CANDIED ORANGE PEEL.

Materials:

1 cup water.   1 cup sugar.
2 cups peel of orange.   Dry sugar.

Way of Preparing:

Cut the peel in long strips and measure two cups of them. Put them in a sauce pan and pour the water over them. Cook until tender. Drain off the water and add the sugar. Gradually heat and when the sugar is melted cook over a slow fire, until the peel is clear. Remove from the fire and when cool dip in dry granulated sugar and pack in jars.

CANDY PUFFS.

Materials:

1 lb. sugar.   1 cup chopped nuts.
1 cup water.   1 teaspoonful flavoring
Whites of 2 eggs.   extract.

Way of Preparing:

Boil the sugar and water until they form a heavy thread. Beat the whites of the eggs very stiff. Pour the syrup slowly over the beaten eggs, stirring all the time. When all the syrup has been used, keep beating until the mass begins to harden, then add the flavoring and nuts, mix thoroughly and place by the spoonful on a greased platter. Make the puffs the size and shape of a large egg.

COCOANUT KISSES.

Materials:

1 fresh cocoanut,   Whites of 2 eggs.
  grated.   ½ teaspoonful flavoring
½ its weight in pow-   extract.
  dered sugar.

Way of Preparing:

Grate the cocoatnut and weigh it, add the sugar, mixing well. Beat the whites of the eggs very stiff, and add them to the grated cocoanut and sugar. Beat the mass hard for five minutes. Add the flavoring extract, then drop it in small spoonfuls on buttered paper, and dry in a slow oven for fifteen minutes.

Quantity:

This will make two dozen kisses.

FONDANT.

Materials:

1 lb. sugar.   ½ cup water.
XXXX sugar.

Way of Preparing:

Boil the sugar until the syrup will spin a heavy thread when dropped into cold water. Carefully pour it out on a large platter. When cool enough to bear your finger in it, stir the mixture rapidly until it is soft, white and creamy. Dust your bread board with XXXX sugar, turn the mixture on it, and knead it as you would biscuit-dough until it is very soft and smooth. It is now ready for use.

Fondant is the basis of all cream candy.

ICE CREAM CANDY.

Materials:

4 cups granulated sugar. 1 tablespoonful glycerine.
½ cup water.   1 teaspoonful flavoring
1 teaspoonful cream of   extract.
   tartar.
½ cup vinegar.

Way of Preparing:

Boil the sugar, water, vinegar and glycerine together, until the mixture will spin a heavy thread. Remove from the fire and when it no longer boils add the cream of tartar and flavoring extract. Pour on a large buttered platter, and when sufficiently cool, pull until white.

Quantity:

This will make two pounds.

MAPLE PUFFS.

Materials:

½ lb. maple sugar.   ½ cup chopped figs.
½ lb. brown sugar.   ½ cup chopped citron.
Whites of 2 eggs.   ½ cup raisins.
1 cup English walnuts. ½ cup water.

Way of Preparing:

Boil the sugar and water until they spin a heavy thread. Beat the whites of the eggs very stiff, gradually add the hot syrup to the whites of the eggs, beating all the time. When the mixture begins to stiffen, add the other ingredients. Beat until it will hold its shape.

Place by tablespoonfuls on greased paper and let stand until stiff.

Quantity:

This will make twelve puffs.

The Wheat Pit in the Chamber of Commerce where quantities of grain are bought and sold for future delivery

Cereals

"Upon my breakfast shall I stay the day"
— WELLINGTON

A DAINTY BREAKFAST DISH.

Materials:

1 cup Pillsbury's Best Cereal.	Salt to taste.
4 cups boiling water.	Cream.
	Sugar.

Way of Preparing:

Stir the Cereal into the boiling water, salt to taste, and boil 15 minutes. Serve with cream and sugar.

Best results are obtained by using the double boiler.

FRIED PILLSBURY'S BEST CEREAL MUSH.

When the Cereal, as in above recipe, is cold, slice it, dip into beaten egg and fry.
Serve with syrup.

BOSTON BROWN BREAD.

Materials:

2¼ cups sour milk.	1 cup Pillsbury's Best.
½ cup molasses.	1 teaspoonful salt.
2 cups Pillsbury's Best Cereal.	1½ level teaspoonfuls soda.

Way of Preparing:

Mix the sour milk, molasses, Cereal, flour, and salt; add the soda, dissolved in one tablespoonful of warm water.

Beat thoroughly, turn into a well-buttered mold and steam four hours.

IDEAL BREAKFAST BREAD.

Materials:

2 eggs.	1 cup Pillsbury's Best Cereal.
1 tablespoonful sugar.	1 cup Pillsbury's Best.
2 cups milk.	1 teaspoonful salt.
3 level teaspoonfuls baking powder.	

Way of Preparing:

Beat the eggs, add the sugar and the milk. Then mix the Cereal, flour, salt and baking powder.

Add first mixture gradually to second mixture, to make a smooth batter. Pour into a well-buttered frying pan. Take one cup milk and pour here and there over the mixture; then bake in a hot oven.

PILLSBURY'S BEST CEREAL SPICED CHOCOLATE CAKE.

Materials:

½ cup butter.	1 teaspoonful allspice.
1½ cups fine granulated sugar.	1 teaspoonful cinnamon. ½ teaspoonful cloves.
Yolks of 3 eggs, well beaten.	1 cup Pillsbury's Best Cereal.
Whites of 3 eggs, beaten until stiff.	½ cup milk. ½ cup water.
2 squares Baker's chocolate, melted.	Beaten whites of 2 eggs. ½ teaspoonful vanilla.
1½ cups Pillsbury's Best. 4 level tablespoonfuls baking powder.	1½ cups sugar boiled for icing.

Way of Preparing:

Cream the half cup of butter, add gradually the granulated sugar, the yolks and whites of the three eggs and the chocolate.

Then mix and sift the flour, baking powder, all-spice, cinnamon and clove, and add the Cereal.

Add to this the first mixture alternately with one-half cup of milk. Bake in layer cake pans and spread between and on top vanilla icing made thus:

Boil 1½ cups sugar with ½ cup water until syrup will thread when dropped from the tip of the spoon. Pour slowly onto the beaten whites of two eggs, and beat until of consistency to spread. Flavor with ½ teaspoonful of vanilla.

PILLSBURY'S BEST CEREAL COFFEE.

Materials:

1 cup Pillsbury's Best Cereal.	5 cups boiling water. Scalded milk or cream.
The white of one egg.	Cut sugar.

Way of Preparing:

Put the Cereal into an iron frying pan, set on top of the range and roast slowly, stirring frequently until the Cereal is of an even golden-brown color. Store in a glass jar. Scald a granite-ware coffee pot that has never been used for ordinary coffee. Moisten ½ cup cereal coffee with the white of the egg.

Turn into coffee pot, and add five cups boiling water.

Let boil thirty minutes, let stand on the back of the range five minutes to settle.

Serve with scalded milk or cream and cut sugar.

Much cheaper than any cereal coffee on the market.

State Inspectors carefully examine and grade every car of wheat arriving in Minneapolis daily

VEAL CROQUETTES.

Materials:

2 cups finely chopped cooked veal.
1 cup Pillsbury's Best Cereal mush.

Salt, pepper and celery salt.
Crumbs and beaten eggs.

Cream sauce made by melting 2 level tablespoonfuls butter, adding 2 level tablespoonfuls flour, and pouring on gradually two-thirds cup of cream.

Way of Preparing:

Mix the chopped veal with the mush, which should be made stiff by using two parts of boiling water to one part of Cereal.

Season highly with salt, pepper and celery salt.

Chill, shape it in cones, dip in egg, crumbs and egg again, and fry in deep fat. Serve with tomato or cream sauce.

PILLSBURY'S BEST CEREAL GEMS.

Materials:

1 cup Pillsbury's Best.
4 level teaspoonfuls baking powder.
2 tablespoonfuls melted butter.

Maple syrup.
½ teaspoonful salt.
½ cup Pillsbury's Best Cereal.
1 cup milk.

Way of Preparing:

Mix and sift the flour, salt and baking powder, then add the Cereal. Beat the yolks of the eggs, add the milk, and combine the mixtures; then add the melted butter and the whites of the eggs, beaten until stiff.

Turn into hot, buttered gem pans and bake in a hot oven twenty-five minutes. Serve with maple syrup.

FRUIT CEREAL.

Materials:

2 cups water boiled with ½ teaspoonful salt.
½ cup Pillsbury's Best Cereal.
5 tablespoonfuls cream.

White of one egg, beaten stiff.
1½ cups berries, strawberries or raspberries preferred.
Whipped cream.

Way of Preparing:

Add gradually to the salted boiling water the half cup of Cereal. Let boil two minutes, then cook in double boiler 30 minutes. Add the cream and cook two minutes. Remove from fire and add the white of one egg, beaten stiff, and the berries.

Breakfast
Grapefruit
Pillsbury's Best Cereal Boiled Eggs
Gems   Coffee

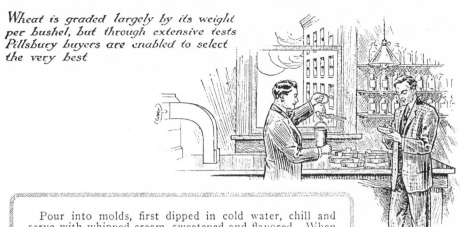

Wheat is graded largely by its weight per bushel, but through extensive tests Pillsbury buyers are enabled to select the very best

Pour into molds, first dipped in cold water, chill and serve with whipped cream, sweetened and flavored. When berries are out of season the Cereal may be molded in individual molds with a teaspoonful of jelly in the bottom of each.

PILLSBURY'S BEST CEREAL GRIDDLE CAKES.

Materials:

4 eggs.	2 cups milk.
4 tablespoonfuls melted butter.	2 cups Pillsbury's Best Cereal Mush.
3 level teaspoonfuls baking powder.	Pillsbury's Best.

Way of Preparing:

Beat the yolks of the eggs until light, add the milk, butter, mush, baking powder, and enough flour to make a stiff batter.

Cut and fold in the whites of four eggs, beaten until stiff. Cook on a hot, well-greased griddle, and serve with maple syrup.

STEAMED PILLSBURY'S BEST CEREAL PUDDING.

Materials:

2 cups scalded milk.	2 tablespoonfuls melted butter.
1 cup Pillsbury's Best Cereal.	1 teaspoonful soda.
½ cup molasses.	1 teaspoonful salt.
2 well beaten eggs.	1 cup seeded raisins (or dates.)

For Sauce:

¼ cup butter.	Grated rind of 1 lemon.
1 cup sugar.	Juice of 2 lemons.
Yolks of two eggs.	

Way of Preparing:

Add gradually to the scalded milk, stirring constantly, the one cup of Cereal. As soon as the mixture thickens, remove from fire and add the molasses, the two beaten eggs, the melted butter, soda, salt and raisins. Dates may be used in place of raisins. Turn into a buttered pudding mold and steam for three hours.

Serve with lemon sauce made thus:

Mix ¼ cup butter, one cup sugar, the yolks of two eggs, and the lemon juice and rind.

Cook on top of double boiler until the mixture thickens, stirring occasionally.

This furnishes a delicious, inexpensive dessert for eight.

39

With a Chafing dish

The chief pleasure in eating does not consist in costly seasoning or exquisite flavor but in yourself

— HORACE

THE use of the chafing dish is, contrary to general opinion, far older than our present civilization. It reaches, in some form, back into the times of the ancient Greeks and Romans.

As used at present, alcohol is the fuel for the lamp attached to it, and a tray is desirable to protect tablecloths and tables from alcohol and fire. The cap covering the opening through which the lamp is filled should be kept in place after filling it. Otherwise, controlling the flame is hardly possible. It is. of course, also possible to connect for heating purposes, with gas and electricity.

Chafing-dish cooking is not done by the average housekeeper.

A chafing-dish needs to be watched carefully from a chair with a high seat to make its use comfortable. For the benefit of the comparatively few, who can and care to indulge in its use, the following recipes are presented.

CREAMED DISHES.

Materials for Cream:

1 cup milk.	1 tablespoonful butter.
1 cup cream.	½ teaspoonful white
1 teaspoonful salt.	pepper.
1 tablespoonful flour.	8 drops onion juice.

Way of Preparing:

Mix cream and milk and bring them to the boiling point. Cream flour and butter together and add to them the salt, pepper and onion juice. Now combine the two mixtures and cook until they have the consistency of thick cream. Remove from the fire. It is ready for use.

Creamed oysters, shrimps, lobster, fish, chicken, turkey, lamb, tongue, dried beef. peas, cauliflower, etc., are made by adding the cooked fish, meat or vegetable to the above cream sauce and the flavor may be varied by adding chopped parsley, celery, salt, curry-powder or lemon juice.

Sweetbreads are particularly good when served in this manner.

OMELETTE.

Materials:

1 tablespoonful water.
3 tablespoonfuls powdered sugar.
1 tablespoonful butter.
½ cup powdered sugar.
¼ teaspoonful salt.
2 large oranges, sliced.
4 eggs.
2 yolks.
Grated rind one orange.
4 tablespoonfuls orange juice.

Way of Preparing:

Beat the yolks of all the eggs until thick; add the sugar, salt, orange juice, and grated rind. Melt the butter in your chafing dish, fold the stiffly-beaten whites of the eggs into the yolk-mixture. When the butter is melted and hot turn the omelette into the dish and cook over the hot water for fifteen minutes. Remove and hold the blazer directly over the flame until the omelette is slightly brown. Extinguish the lamp and serve the omelette directly from the blazer.

When serving, garnish the omelette with the sliced orange and dust with the powdered sugar.

Quantity:

This will serve four people.

OYSTER STEW.

Materials:

1 cup milk.
½ cup cream.
½ teaspoonful salt.
2 dozen oysters.
1 heaping tablespoonful butter.
¼ teaspoonful pepper.
¼ cup cracker crumbs.

Way of Preparing:

Melt the butter in the chafing dish and add the milk, cream and seasonings. When boiling hot add the oysters. Cook them until they look plump. Add the cracker crumbs and serve.

Quantity:

This will serve four persons.

PEACH SANDWICHES.

Materials:

1 stale sponge cake.
1 can of peaches.
2 tablespoonfuls butter.
½ cup sherry wine.
½ cup sugar.
½ teaspoonful powdered cinnamon.
Grated rind one orange.
1 pint whipped cream.

Samples of wheat are milled through a complete system of miniature machines and the flour fully tested to determine their essential properties

Way of Preparing:

Slice the sponge cake into one-half inch slices. Stamp out with a fancy cutter twice as many round pieces as you have persons to serve. Melt the butter in your chafing dish and brown in it the pieces of cut-out sponge cake. Remove them to a platter, drain the peaches, having as many halves of peaches as you have pieces of sponge cake. To the butter in your chafing dish add the sugar, sherry and grated orange peel. When these ingredients are hot add the drained peaches. Cook five minutes. Extinguish the lamp and prepare to serve. When serving place on a small plate one round of sponge cake, on this place one-half a peach, on top of this peach place another round of sponge cake and put another half peach on top of the latter. Dust with a pinch of cinnamon and garnish with whipped cream.

Quantity:

Serve one sandwich to each person.

TAPIOCA AND GRAPE JUICE PUDDING.

Materials:

1 cup grape juice.	Pinch of salt.
1 cup water.	Stiffly beaten whites of three
1 cup sugar.	eggs.
¼ cup minute tapioca.	Cream.
Juice of two lemons.	

Way of Preparing:

Soak the tapioca for fifteen minutes in the cup of water. Place in a chafing dish and add the sugar. When hot add the grape juice. Cook until the tapioca is transparent. Then add the lemon juice and salt. Lastly fold in the beaten whites of the eggs.

Serve either hot or cold with plain cream.

Quantity:

This will serve six persons.

Luncheon
Plain Omelette   Cream Potatoes
Peanut Butter Sandwiches
Tapioca Pudding   Tea

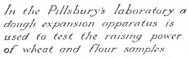

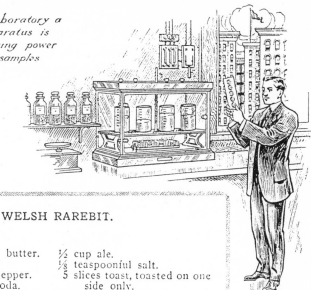

WELSH RAREBIT.

Materials:

1 tablespoonful butter.
1 egg.
⅛ teaspoonful pepper.
¼ teaspoonful soda.
½ lb. cheese.

½ cup ale.
⅛ teaspoonful salt.
5 slices toast, toasted on one side only.

Way of Preparing:

Melt the butter in your chafing dish and then add the cheese broken into small pieces; stir without stopping until the cheese is melted. Add the egg, beaten and diluted with the ale, lastly add the salt, pepper and soda.

Serve immediately on the toast with the untoasted side up.

Cream may be substituted for the ale if desired.

Quantity:

This will serve five people.

SARDINE RAREBIT.

⅛ teaspoonful Extract of Beef.
1 Box good sardines.
½ teaspoonful salt.

2 tablespoonsful grated cheese.
1 tablespoonful thick cream.
2 eggs, yolks.
6 teaspoonsful melted butter.

Way of Preparing:

Remove bones and skins and pound meat to a paste. Add a few drops of onion juice, and lemon juice, a dash of salt, two tablespoonfuls of grated cheese and one tablespoonful of thick cream. Toast narrow strips of bread on one side. Spread the sardine mixture on the untoasted sides, cover with the other strip and set in the oven until the sauce is made. Beat the yolks of two eggs. Add to them six teaspoonfuls of melted butter and the Beef Extract. Stand on the fire to heat until it begins to thicken. Add one-half teaspoonful of salt and a dash of paprika. Turn this mixture on the strips which have been kept hot in the oven. Serve at once with quarters of lemon.

Egg Dishes

"Oh eggs, within thine oval shell,
What palate-tickling joys do dwell."

IT takes no Christopher Columbus to discover that eggs have two advantages over all other foods. First, they are procurable nearly everywhere; second, the most dainty person is sure when eating eggs that they have not been handled. They possess their highest nourishing value in their raw state, and the longer an egg is subject to heat the harder it is to digest.

Eggs are digested more readily when the whites and yolks are thoroughly mixed before cooking, therefore in a scrambled state and as omelettes they are the easiest digested. Eggs are at their very best when only twelve hours old. A fresh egg feels heavy and sinks flatly to the bottom in water. They may be kept for months by packing them small ends down in ordinary coarse salt. Each should stand upright and not touch another.

EGG CROQUETTES.

Materials:

¼ cup butter.
½ cup Pillsbury's Best.
1 egg.
¼ teaspoonful pepper.
1 tablespoonful chopped parsley.
*½ cup white stock.

½ cup cream.
½ teaspoonful salt.
8 hard boiled eggs.
1 teaspoonful onion juice.
1 pint parboiled oysters.

Way of Preparing:

Make a sauce with the butter, flour, cream, stock, uncooked egg, well beaten, the salt and pepper. Then add to it the cooked whites of eggs, chopped fine and the yolks passed through a vegetable press. Lastly add the chopped parsley and the onion juice. Let this mixture get cold, then form into egg-shaped croquettes with an oyster in the center of each. Now egg, crumb and fry them in deep fat. Garnish with parsley when serving.

Quantity:

This will serve six.

*"White Stock" will be found under "Soups."

EGGS WITH CREAM DRESSING.

Materials:

2 tablespoonfuls butter.	1 teaspoonful salt.
3 tablespoonfuls flour.	Few grains pepper.
1½ cups milk.	3 hard boiled eggs.

Way of Preparing:

Blend butter and flour. Place on the range and stir until butter is melted. Add milk, stirring all the time till mixture is thick. Add salt and pepper. Separate the whites of the eggs from the yolks. Chop the whites fine, and add to the dressing. Arrange slices of toast on a hot platter, pour the dressing over them; force the yolks through a ricer onto the toast and dressing; serve hot.

OMELETTE.

Omelettes are of two classes: The French and the puffy. There are many variations, but all belong to one of the two classes.

The number of yolks should exceed the number of whites in an omelette. If this rule is observed they will be more tender and of a looser texture.

PLAIN OMELETTE.

Materials:

3 eggs.	2 tablespoonfuls clear bacon
½ teaspoonful salt.	fat or 1 tablespoonful
Dash of pepper.	butter.
	3 tablespoonfuls hot water.

Way of Preparing:

Beat eggs very light, add salt, pepper and hot water. Heat the omelette pan, and add bacon fat or butter. Cook slowly. When thickened and browned underneath, put in grate of oven to finish the top. When the top will not adhere to the finger, the omelette is done. Fold and serve on hot platter.

Quantity:

Will serve four people.

An electric furnace is used by Pillsbury's chemists when uniform temperatures are required in making ash determinations

FRENCH OMELETTE.

Materials:

4 eggs.	Pinch pepper.
5 tablespoonfuls ice water.	1 teaspoonful sugar.
½ teaspoonful salt.	1 heaping tablespoonful butter.
2 egg yolks.	

Way of Preparing:

Place the eggs in a bowl and beat with a fork until they are thoroughly mixed and then strain them, add the water, salt, pepper and sugar. Melt the butter in a frying pan, pour in the egg mixture. Set over the fire for a minute, then with a spatula separate the cooked portion from the frying pan and gently move it back and forth so that the uncooked portions may come in contact with the pan. When it becomes creamy and begins to set, begin at the side of the pan, next to the handle, with a spatula, and fold the omelette over. Turn onto a hot platter and serve immediately.

Quantity:

This will serve four people.

HYGIENIC EGGS.

Materials:

6 eggs.	*½ cup white sauce.
6 round slices of toast.	Salt and pepper.
1 cup finely-chopped chicken.	

Way of Preparing:

Heat the chicken in the sauce and spread each slice of toast with the mixture. Beat the whites of the eggs until very stiff, pile the beaten whites on the rounds of toast in the shape of nests. Carefully place one unbroken yolk in each nest. Cook in a moderate oven until set. Dust with salt and pepper and serve at once.

Quantity:

This will serve six.

*Recipe for white sauce will be found under "White Sauce Omelette."

Breakfast
Oranges
Pillsbury's Best Cereal Mush
(Cooked all night in Fireless Cooker)
Scrambled Eggs
Rolls   Coffee

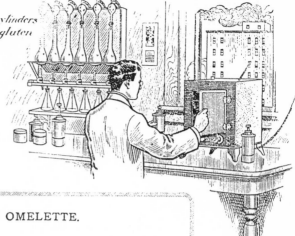

PUFF OMELETTE.

Materials:

4 eggs.	6 tablespoonfuls water.
2 yolks.	½ teaspoonful salt.
Pinch pepper.	1 tablespoonful butter.

Way of Preparing:

Beat the whites of the eggs until dry and the yolks until they are thick and of a lemon color. Add the water, salt and pepper to the yolks. Mix thoroughly and then fold the whites into the yolk mixture. Put the butter in a frying pan and when it is hot put in the mixture. Let it stand in a moderate heat for two minutes, place in a hot oven and cook until set. Remove from the oven, cut across the center at right angles to the handle, turn on a hot platter and serve.

Quantity:

This will serve four persons.

Note.—Either French or puff omelette may be varied by the use of fillings, or garnishings, or both.

SCRAMBLED EGGS.

Materials:

6 eggs.	½ teaspoonful salt.
2 tablespoonfuls milk.	¼ teaspoonful white pepper.
2 tablespoonfuls water.	2 tablespoonfuls butter.

Way of Preparing:

Beat the eggs without separating, add the other ingredients, mixing thoroughly. Strain the mixture. Melt the butter in a frying pan and pour in the mixture. Stir constantly until it is soft and creamy throughout.

Serve at once.

This dish may be varied by the addition of any finely chopped cooked meat. If so, it should be mixed with the eggs just before taking from the fire.

Quantity:

This will serve four persons.

FIRELESS COOKING.

THE principle upon which this new-old device works is, that a dish started cooking over a fire, will, if set into a tightly closed, insulated box, continue to cook by its own heat until it is done, with no further application of fire.

Not only is this principle correct, but in actual practice the fireless cooker, when rightly used, has proved most successful in every phase of cookery, viz., roasting, frying, baking and boiling. It can be used in cooking soups, meats, fish, sauces, fruits, pies, etc., and with the following advantages.

There is a saving in fuel—for after the initial short cooking no more fuel is needed. Less costly cuts of meat and older fowls may be used and rendered nutritious and palatable by the fireless. Again, from a given quantity of raw material there is less waste in cooking. Moreover you need no longer spend your day in a hot, smelly kitchen. Start your evening meal in the morning, place it in the fireless cooker, and, with no fear that your meal will burn or overdo, go about your business—to your sewing, your reading, to the children, or to the theater; returning neither irritated nor worried to a clean, sweet smelling kitchen (for there are no odors with the fireless) to find your meal perfectly cooked and ready to set on the table.

There are two general types of fireless cookers on the market; those with and without "radiators" of iron or soapstone which are heated by themselves and placed in the cooker with the heated food. Where radiators are used it is possible to impart some degree of crispness to the food and to maintain a higher degree of heat for a longer period of time than is possible in the radiatorless type.

Realizing that radiator fireless cooker is a practical and valuable kitchen adjunct, Pillsbury's,—ever in the forefront of Progress—presents on the opposite page directions by which the recipes given in this book may be adapted to the use of the fireless cooker.

Bread and Biscuits.

In baking Bread or Biscuits in the Fireless Cooker, proceed in the ordinary way with your favorite recipe, when ready to bake, heat two radiators sizzling hot (test with wet finger) and placing in cooker well with the bread, allow to cook as long as would be necessary in the ordinary hot oven. In the case of bread this should be about one hour and fifteen minutes. For Buns and Biscuits from fifteen to twenty minutes. Hot radiators insure nice, crisp brown crust and thorough cooking, with no danger of burning.

48

FIRELESS COOKING.

Cakes.

Cakes should be baked in the cooker with moderately hot discs for about the same length of time as is customary with an oven. For instance, Sponge Cake, for from forty minutes to one hour.

Cereals.

In cooking Pillsbury's Cereal, Oat Meal or any other cereal, boil slowly over the fire for five to ten minutes, after which place the dish in the cooker over night. Because of the long cooking, cereals take more water with the Fireless than when cooked in the ordinary manner.

Fish.

Fish will be found deliciously baked if placed in the cooker with two hot discs for about forty minutes.

Meats.

To roast in the Fireless Cooker, prepare the meat (Roast Leg of Lamb, Roast Fowl, Pot Roast) in the usual manner. Heat the roaster well of the Cooker by placing one hot radiator therein. When well is warm remove the now-cool radiator and set in the roast with two very hot discs. Close Cooker quickly and tightly.

Pot Roast or Roast Lamb should remain in the Cooker from six to ten hours while an old fowl should roast from eight to twelve hours.

Boiled Meat should be placed over the fire until it is thoroughly heated to its very center, or about thirty minutes according to the size of the meat. Place quickly in the Fireless with or without radiator for from six to eight hours.

Pastry.

Place pies with hot discs into cooker and leave for about the same time as ordinary cooking in a hot oven demands.

Soups.

Soups should be prepared according to recipes given in this book, brought to boiling point over a flame and allowed to boil slowly for from ten minutes in the case of Brown Soup Stock to thirty minutes in the case of White Soup Stock. After which it is quickly placed in the Fireless and left for eight hours.

Vegetables.

Potatoes and other starchy vegetables should be brought to a smart boil over the fire and placed in the Fireless with two very hot radiators for about the same time as is customary on the stove. Parsnips, carrots and turnips with a small percentage of starch should be cooked more slowly with cooker discs.

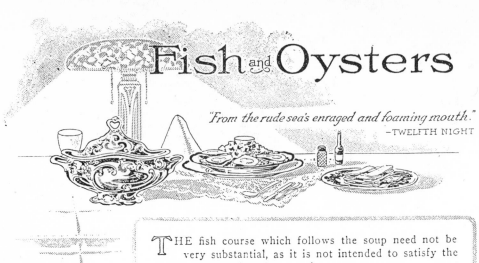

Fish and Oysters

"From the rude sea's enraged and foaming mouth."

—TWELFTH NIGHT

THE fish course which follows the soup need not be very substantial, as it is not intended to satisfy the hunger but to whet the appetite.

It may consist of any fish, boiled or baked, fish-cutlets, small fish fried or planked fish.

Shell-fish may also be served at this point of the dinner, as lobsters boiled, soft shell crabs, boiled or fried, oysters raw and raw clams.

Potatoes in some form are always served with fish, and either raw cucumbers, tomatoes or radishes are passed.

If the fish is served with sauce, potatoes should be offered, fried in some form such as croquettes, cakes or straws.

In serving fish at dinner the light-meated ones are preferred, because they are more easily digested than those with dark meat.

BAKED FISH.

Materials:

4 lbs. fish.	2 tablespoonfuls grated
1 tablespoonful salt.	onion.
1 pint bread crumbs.	¼ teaspoonful pepper.
4 tablespoonfuls melted	½ teaspoonful salt.
butter.	1 cup raw oysters.
1 lemon.	Slices of fat pork.
1 tablespoonful minced	
parsley.	

Way of Preparing:

Have a four-pound fish, with the head on; wash it thoroughly, and sprinkle with one tablespoonful of salt. Put in the ice box and leave it there two hours.

Make a stuffing of one cup of crumbs, the parsley, grated onion, melted butter, lemon juice, grated rind of lemon, salt, pepper and raw oysters chopped.

Fill the body of the fish with this stuffing, sew up the opening and skewer into any desired shape. Place on a baking sheet, cover with slices of fat pork and bake in a hot oven.

When the fish begins to brown baste it with hot water and reduce the heat of the oven.

Bake slowly, basting every ten minutes. At the end of forty minutes remove the pork, cover the fish with a white sauce, sprinkle with bread crumbs and bake until the crumbs are brown. When done remove to a hot platter and garnish with fried oysters, parsley, or slices of lemon and parsley.

Quantity:

This will serve six people.

BROILED LOBSTER.

Materials:

1 live lobster.   Sliced lemon.
½ cup melted butter.

Way of Preparing:

Begin at the mouth of the lobster and with a sharp knife split the lobster through the body and tail.

Open and remove the liver, stomach and intestinal vein. Brush the lobster well with melted butter. Put on the broiler, flesh-side up, and broil ten minutes.

Turn shell-side and broil eight minutes. Serve with melted butter and sliced lemon.

Quantity:

This will serve two persons.

CODFISH BALLS.

Materials:

1 cup cooked codfish.   1 cup mashed potatoes pre-
2 eggs.   pared as for the table.
1 cup cracker crumbs.   Flour.
Fat.   Fried potatoes.
                                         Parsley.

Mash the codfish very smooth. Add the potatoes and one egg well beaten, and mix thoroughly. Form into small balls about the size of an English walnut. Roll in flour, then in egg, then in cracker crumbs, and fry in deep fat.

Drain, pile on a platter in a nice pyramid. garnish with fried potatoes and parsley and serve.

Quantity:

This will serve five persons.

Accurate analytical balances used in making extensive tests in our chemical laboratory

CREAMED FISH.

Materials:

2 cups cold fish.	2 tablespoonfuls flour.
1 cup hot milk.	½ teaspoonful salt.
1 bay leaf.	¼ teaspoonful white pepper.
½ teaspoonful onion juice.	½ cup fine crumbs.
2 tablespoonfuls butter.	

Way of Preparing:

Make a sauce by creaming the flour and butter and adding them to the hot milk. Put this in a double boiler and add the salt, pepper, onion juice and bay leaf. Stir until as thick as cream. Now cover the bottom of a baking dish with some of the cold fish, flaked, and pour over it half the sauce. Then put in another layer of fish and on that pour the remainder of the sauce.

Sprinkle all with crumbs, dot with butter and brown in a moderately hot oven.

Any kind of cold fish may be used.

Quantity:

This will serve six persons.

CURRIED LOBSTER.

Materials:

2 two-pound lobsters.	1 tablespoonful flour.
2 teaspoonfuls lemon juice.	1 cup scalded milk.
½ teaspoonful curry powder.	1 cup cracker crumbs.
	½ teaspoonful salt.
2 tablespoonfuls butter.	¼ teaspoonful pepper.

Way of Preparing:

Cream the butter and flour and add the scalded milk, then add the lemon juice, curry powder, salt and pepper. Remove the lobster meat from the shells and cut into half-inch cubes. Add the latter to the sauce. Refill the lobster shells, cover with buttered crumbs, and bake until the crumbs are brown. Instead of the shells you may use a buttered baking dish.

Quantity:

This will serve six persons.

Luncheon
Fish Croquettes with Tomato Sauce
Corn Meal Muffins   Rice Pudding
Tea

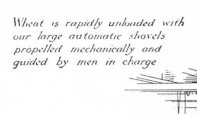

FISH CHOWDER.

Materials:

2½ lbs. fresh fish, sliced.   ½ lb. salt pork.
4 large potatoes, sliced.   1 large onion.
1 cup milk.   3 sea biscuits.

Way of Preparing:

Cut the pork in cubes and put them in a frying pan over the fire. When they are frying put in the onion sliced, and fry it brown. Butter a small kettle and put in a layer of the sliced potatoes, then one of fish, then a layer of pork and onions. Sprinkle with salt and pepper. Put in another layer of potatoes, one of fish, one of pork and onions, sprinkle again with salt and pepper, and put in one more layer of potatoes. Pour over all the milk and enough water to nearly cover it. Now place the cover on the kettle and let it boil slowly for twenty-five minutes. Remove the cover and place on top of the chowder two or three sea-biscuits, broken in pieces. Replace the cover and let the chowder barely simmer ten minutes longer. Then serve immediately.

Quantity:

This will serve eight persons.

Note.—Oyster and clam chowder are prepared in the same manner.

FISH CROQUETTES.

Materials:

2 cups cold fish.   2 tablespoonfuls flour.
1 cup milk.   2 tablespoonfuls butter.
1 teaspoonful salt.   ½ teaspoonful pepper.
1 cup crumbs.   2 eggs.
Parsley.   Lemons.
Fat.

Way of Preparing:

Cream the flour and butter. Put the milk in a double boiler, and when it is at the boiling point add the flour and butter. Stir until it is smooth and thick, and add the salt, pepper and fish, flaked. Spread on a platter and let it cool. Then shape, roll in flour, egg and crumbs and fry in deep fat. Arrange on a hot dish, and garnish with parsley and sliced lemon.

Quantity:

This will serve six persons.

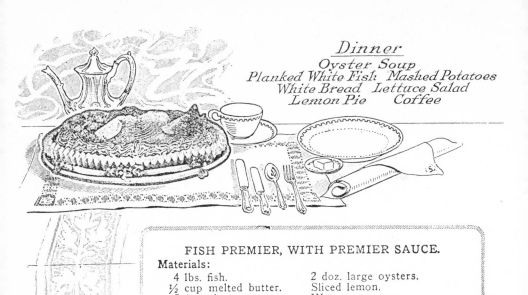

FISH PREMIER, WITH PREMIER SAUCE.

Materials:

4 lbs. fish.	2 doz. large oysters.
½ cup melted butter.	Sliced lemon.
Salt and pepper.	Watercress.
1 cup crumbs.	

Way of Preparing:

Remove the head and tail of the fish. Skin and bone it, leaving two oblong pieces. Lay one of the pieces on a greased baking sheet in the baking pan, cover with half of the oysters. Sprinkle thickly with crumbs and pour over them one-half of your melted butter. Then cover it with the other half of the fish. Place the remaining oysters on top of the fish, sprinkle with salt and pepper. Place the remaining crumbs on the oysters and pour the rest of the butter over the crumbs. Put into a moderate oven and brown. When done slip it carefully onto a hot platter, garnish with watercress and sliced lemon, and serve with a

Premier Sauce,

made of—

¼ cup of butter.	¼ teaspoonful salt.
Yolk of one egg.	⅓ cup boiling water.
Juice of ½ lemon.	A pinch of white pepper.

Cook in a double boiler for six minutes and serve in a sauceboat.

Quantity:

This will easily serve six persons.

LOBSTER, NEWBURG STYLE.

Materials:

2 large lobsters, boiled.	1 wineglass sherry wine.
½ teaspoonful salt.	½ pint cream.
¼ teaspoonful white pepper.	3 egg yolks.
	2 tablespoonfuls butter.
2 large truffles, slice.	Toast.

Way of Preparing:

Cut the lobster meat in inch pieces, put them in a saucepan with the butter, and place over a hot fire. Add the salt, pepper and truffles, and cook five minutes. Then add the sherry and cook three minutes longer.

Beat the yolks of the eggs and whip them into the cream, now add this slowly to the lobster and cook three minutes. Serve on toast.

Quantity:
This will serve eight persons.

PLANKED FISH.

Materials:

4 lbs. white fish.	½ cup butter.
1 lemon.	½ teaspoonful pepper.
1 teaspoonful salt.	1 cup boiling water.

Way of Preparing:

Remove the head from the fish and have it split from head to tail, so that it can be flattened out on the plank. Take care not to split the skin. Have the plank very hot and brush with butter. Place the fish, skin-side down on the board and tack it firmly in place.

Put it in a moderately hot oven and at the end of five minutes take a small brush and give the fish a bath, using the other ingredients, which you have made into a sauce for basting. Continue this every ten minutes for thirty-five minutes. Then remove from the oven, place the plank on a platter and serve at once. Garnish the platter so as to cover the plank, but never remove the fish from it when serving.

The plank should be of hardwood (oak) sixteen inches long, twelve inches wide and one and a half inches thick.

Quantity:
This dish will serve six persons.

PIGS IN BLANKETS.

Materials:

Large oysters.	Pepper.
Thin slices of breakfast bacon.	Toothpicks.
	Celery.
Lemon.	Toast.
Melted butter.	

Way of Preparing:

Wash and dry the oysters. Have as many strips of bacon as you have oysters. Place a strip of bacon lengthwise on your left hand, lay an oyster across the upper end. Now begin to roll toward the tips of your fingers. When the oyster is inclosed in the bacon, skewer the latter with a small toothpick. When you have prepared all the oysters in this manner, sprinkle with pepper, dip in the melted butter and broil. Serve on hot toast with celery, and garnish the platter with lemon and the white leaves of the celery.

Quantity:
Allow four to each person.

Receiving the wheat through the great steel car pits and conveying it on fast running belts to elevators

Game

Let's carve him as a dish fit for the gods,
Not hew him as a carcass.
— JULIUS CAESAR

SINCE the days of Nimrod, the first hunter, every household has been stirred to its foundation every now and then by a male member stalking in with some wild thing "plucked from the forest" and demanding that "you cook it."

Then it is that the faithful wife trembles with emotion. All eyes are upon her. Her ability in the estimation of her husband will rise or fall with that goose.

BROILED QUAIL.

Materials:

Quail.	Salt.
Melted butter.	Pepper.
Lemon.	Parsley.
Currant jelly.	Toast.

Way of Preparing:

Singe and wipe clean; beginning at the neck on the back, split and lay open. Remove the inside contents, then remove the breastbone and wipe clean inside. Sprinkle with salt and pepper, brush with melted butter, and broil for fifteen minutes on a brisk fire. Turn frequently. When done serve, garnished with parsley on toast or with currant jelly.

BROILED VENISON STEAK.

Materials:

Venison steak.	Pepper.
Butter.	Salt.

Way of Preparing:

Wipe the steak with a cloth wrung out of cold water. Place the steak in a hot buttered broiler and broil with a clear brisk fire. Turn every ten seconds for the first minute. After that turn occasionally until cooked on both sides.

Venison should always be served rare. Roast venison is prepared the same as roast lamb.

56

ROAST WILD DUCK.

Materials:

1 wild duck.   Salt and pepper.
4 strips salt pork.   Currant jelly.
½ cup water.

Way of Preparing:

Clean and truss the duck and sprinkle with salt and pepper. Cover the breast with the slices of salt pork. Place on the rack in the dripping pan and pour the water in the pan. Put in a hot oven and cook half an hour, basting every five minutes with the drippings from the pan. Remove the bacon and serve with currant jelly.

Domestic Duck

is cooked in the same manner, but requires one hour and a quarter of cooking.

Stuffing

is used the same as for chicken or turkey or you may stuff with apples, peeled and cut in eighths. If no stuffing is used, a whole onion placed in the body of the duck while cooking, will improve the flavor and should be removed before serving.

Roast Partridge (Grouse, Pheasant, Quail, Prairie Chicken etc.)

Do not cut off head until game is ready to dress. Scald in boiling hot water so the feathers may be plucked easily without the skin being torn. Draw carefully, wiping out with a clean wet cloth. Part of the gamey taste may be removed if desired, by soaking it in salt and water before placing in oven, strips of salt pork or bacon may be scured, separately from side to side, across the breast. In baking, baste from four to six minutes. Thick slices of toast may be placed under each bird in the pan before taking out and so served. Coarse bread crumbs, fried brown in butter, may be sprinkled over the bird on platter before being brought to the table, bread sauce or brown gravy may also be used, as well as two or three tablespoonfuls of butter, put into the dressed bird. When liver is used, cut up and roll same to a paste, and mix with butter, salt, pepper and spread on the toast.

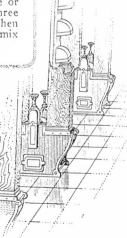

Screw conveyors and endless cup elevators by which the wheat and its products are carried through the Pillsbury's Mills

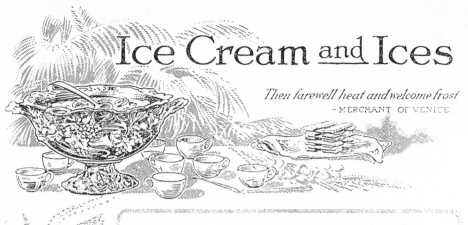

Ice Cream and Ices

Then farewell heat and welcome frost

— MERCHANT OF VENICE

ICE creams are divided into two different classes; the Neapolitan and the Philadelphian. The former contains a large proportion of eggs, has a pronounced custard flavor and its color is lemon-yellow. The Philadelphian has a creamy shade and the flavor of sweet cream.

The first operation in making either kind is the cooking, either with or without eggs. In case of the Neapolitan, strain the yolks of the eggs and beat until thick and lemon-colored, then add the sugar and beat again. Then add the stiffly-beaten whites and beat again. Add the milk and cream and cook in a double boiler until it coats a spoon without running. Stir constantly and be careful not to let it curdle. Strain again through a wine sieve and let it cool. Flavoring is added either before or after cooking. This depends upon the kind of flavor used, but the process thus far is the same with all Neapolitan creams.

The Philadelphian cream is sometimes made of fresh, uncooked cream, if a very light, fluffy cream is wanted. Cook the cream in a double boiler, with cold water in the outer pan. Bring to a boil, and then remove from the fire. Add the flavoring and the sugar and stir until the latter is melted. Strain and cool. Now it is ready for the freezer.

In adding fruit to the creams (such as peaches, pineapple, plums, oranges or apricots) it must be cut into small dice, sprinkled with sugar and allowed to stand two hours.

Berries must be mashed, sugared and mixed with the frozen cream. Always thoroughly chill the cream before freezing it. It is then smoother and the chilling makes it freeze more rapidly and easily.

FREEZING.

Pour the chilled cream into the freezer. Place the freezer in the pail and pack with ice nearly to the top. Sprinkle coarse salt uniformly on the ice as you pack it into the bucket. Cover and fasten the can and turn it slowly until it becomes difficult to turn. Open the can and remove the dasher.

Scrape the cream from the sides of the can. Mix until smooth, close the can and drain off the brine. Add fresh ice and salt, covering the entire can. Wrap a blanket around the freezer and let it stand two hours.

In very hot weather renew the salt and ice three times and keep the blanket cold and wet with the brine from the freezer.

ANGEL FOOD ICE CREAM.

Materials:

Whites of four eggs.   1 quart whipped cream.
½ cup sugar.   1 teaspoonful almond extract.

Way of Preparing:

Beat the eggs very stiff and stir in the sugar, fold in the whipped cream and the flavoring extract. Line a mold with New York ice cream* and fill the center with this mixture.

Pack in salt and ice and let it stand three hours.

Quantity:

This will serve six persons.

*The recipe for New York ice cream you will find elsewhere herein.

BURNT ALMOND ICE CREAM.

Materials:

1 quart cream.   4 oz. shelled almonds.
6 eggs.   1 tablespoonful vanilla.
1 lb. sugar.

Way of Preparing:

Blanch the almonds and brown them in the oven. Pound to a paste in a mortar, adding a little sugar and cream to make a paste.

Mix the eggs, sugar and cream, and add the almond paste. Then freeze according to directions under "Freezing." Adding a tablespoonful of Caramel will produce a richer color.

Quantity:

This will serve six persons.

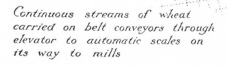

Continuous streams of wheat carried on belt conveyors through elevator to automatic scales on its way to mills

CARAMEL ICE CREAM.

Materials:

1 quart cream.
6 eggs.
1 lb. sugar.

1 tablespoonful vanilla extract.
4 tablespoonfuls caramel.

Way of Preparing:

Prepare the custard as directed. Freeze as per directions for "Freezing" and add the caramel and vanilla when beating down the half frozen cream.

Quantity:

This will serve six persons.

CHESTNUT ICE CREAM.

Materials:

1 pint cream.
1 pint milk.
6 eggs.
1 lb. sugar.

4 oz. chestnut meats.
2 tablespoonfuls vanilla extract.

Way of Preparing:

Use the Italian chestnuts. Boil them until soft. Peel and reduce them to a pulp in a mortar, adding a little sugar and cream enough to form a paste.

Prepare the sugar, eggs and cream and add the chestnut paste. Then cook and freeze as directed under "Freezing."

Quantity:

This will serve eight persons.

CHOCOLATE ICE CREAM.

Materials:

1 pint cream.
1 pint milk.
6 eggs.
5 ozs. chocolate.

¾ lb. sugar.
1 teaspoonful cinnamon extract.

Way of Preparing:

Melt the chocolate and add the cinnamon extract. Make and cook the custard as directed in general remarks on Ice Creams; then add to it the chocolate while both are hot. Cool, chill and freeze as directed in "Freezing." To make

Caramel Chocolate Ice Cream

omit the cinnamon extract and use instead three tablespoonfuls of the prepared caramel syrup, recipe for which you will find elsewhere in this volume.

Quantity:

This will serve six persons.

Luncheon
Cream of Celery Soup
Scrambled Eggs   Corn Bread
Nesselrode Pudding
Tea

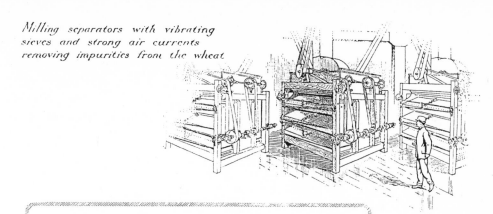

Milling separators with vibrating sieves and strong air currents removing impurities from the wheat

COFFEE ICE CREAM.

Materials:

1 quart cream.   1 cup ground coffee.
1 quart milk.   1 teaspoonful vanilla extract.
9 eggs.   Whipped cream.
1½ lbs. sugar.

Way of Preparing:

Pour the milk over the coffee and bring to a boil. Boil slowly ten minutes and then allow it to settle and cool. Drain off the milk and strain it, add enough more milk to make one quart. Add this to the cream, eggs and sugar, make a custard as explained elsewhere herein, and freeze according to directions in "Freezing." Serve with whipped cream.

Quantity:

This will serve ten persons.

MAPLE PERFECT.

Materials:

4 eggs.   1 teaspoonful almond extract.
½ pint hot maple syrup.   Salt and ice.
1 pint thick cream.

Way of Preparing:

Beat the eggs slightly and pour on them slowly the maple syrup. Cook until the mixture thickens and cool it, then add the extract, remove from the range, cool, and then add the cream, beaten until stiff. Mold, pack in salt and ice and let stand four hours.

Quantity:

This will serve six persons.

NESSELRODE PUDDING.

Materials:

3 cups cream.   2 cups milk.
2 cups sugar.   ½ cup pineapple syrup.
5 egg yolks.   1 pint prepared Italian
1 pinch salt.   chestnuts.
½ cup Sultana raisins.   1 cup candied fruits.

Way of Preparing:

Make a custard of the milk, sugar, eggs and salt, according to directions elsewhere herein, strain and cool. Add the pineapple syrup, cream and chestnuts. Then freeze, as directed elsewhere herein. Line a two-quart mold with part of the mixture and to the remainder add one cup candied fruits, minced, one-half cup sultana raisins and six chestnuts, chopped.

Fill the mold. Pack in ice, and let it stand three hours. To "prepare" the chestnuts, shell and boil until very soft, then pass them through a potato ricer.

Quantity:
This will serve twelve persons.

NEW YORK ICE CREAM.

Materials:

2 cups milk.	1 tablespoonful vanilla extract.
3 cups cream.	
1 cup sugar.	1 tablespoonful lemon extract.
1 pinch salt.	
Yolks of 7 eggs.	Warm water.
1 tablespoonful gelatine.	

Way of Preparing:
Make a custard of the milk, sugar, eggs and salt. Bring it to a boil. Remove from the fire and add the gelatine, melted in a little warm water, cool, strain and flavor. Whip the cream, add it to the custard and freeze according to directions elsewhere herein.

Quantity:
This will serve eight persons.

NOUGAT ICE CREAM.

Materials:

2 cups milk.	5 egg whites.
1 cup sugar.	¼ cup filberts.
5 egg yolks.	¼ cup English walnuts.
½ teaspoonful salt.	¼ cup almond meats.
2 cups thick cream.	¼ cup hickory nuts.
1 tablespoonful vanilla extract.	1 teaspoonful almond extract.
¼ cup pistachios.	

Way of Preparing:
Make a custard of the milk, sugar, egg yolks and salt, as per directions elsewhere herein, and strain and cool. Beat the cream and add it. Then add the nut-meats chopped fine, the whites of the eggs, well-beaten and the flavoring extracts. Freeze according to directions elsewhere herein, and allow it to stand four hours.

Quantity:
This will serve ten persons.

Dinner
Oxtail Soup
Pot Roast Beef
Browned Potatoes
Salt Rising Bread
Pineapple Ice
Coffee

Pepper Grass.   Wild Oats.   Wild Buckwheat. Inferior Wheat.   Mustard Seed.   Screenings.

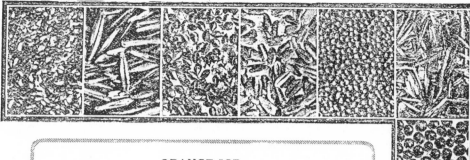

Wild Peas.

ORANGE ICE.

Materials:

1 pint orange juice.
1 quart water.
1 pint sugar.
Serve in glasses.

Grated rind of one lemon.
¼ pint lemon juice.
Grated rind of one orange.

Way of Preparing:

Freeze (according to directions elsewhere herein) and Make a syrup of the sugar and water. Boil fifteen minutes and add the orange juice, lemon juice, orange peel and lemon rind.

Quantity:

This will serve twelve persons.

PINEAPPLE MOUSSE.

Materials:

1 tablespoonful granu-
   lated gelatine.
¼ cup cold water.
1 cup pineapple syrup.

2 tablespoonfuls lemon
   juice.
1½ cups sugar.
1 quart whipped cream.

Way of Preparing:

Soak the gelatine in the cold water. Heat the pineapple syrup and add the lemon juice, sugar and gelatine; strain and cool. When the mixture thickens fold in the whipped cream. Mold, pack in salt and ice and let stand four hours.

Quantity:

This will serve six persons.

PINEAPPLE ICE.

Materials:

4 cups water.
2 cups sugar.
Juice of 6 lemons.

4 cups ice water.
1 can grated pineapple.

Way of Preparing:

Make a syrup of the water and sugar and boil for fifteen minutes. Add the pineapple and lemon juice. Cool and add the icewater. Freeze until mushy, using half ice and half salt.

Quantity:
This will serve twelve persons.

PISTACHIO ICE CREAM.

Materials:

1 quart cream.	1 oz. bitter almonds.
6 eggs.	1 teaspoonful vanilla extract.
1 lb. sugar.	Rosewater.
4 oz. pistachio nuts.	

Way of Preparing:

Pound the nuts in a mortar and add a few drops of
rosewater. Gradually add one cup of cream and one of
sugar. Mix all the ingredients, cook as per general directions herein and freeze as directed under "Freezing."

Quantity:
This will serve six persons.

ROMAN PUNCH.

Materials:

*2 quarts pineapple ice.	4 whites of eggs.
½ pint Jamaica rum.	2 tablespoonfuls vanilla.
½ lb. sugar.	1 pint champagne.

Way of Preparing:

Put the sugar in a saucepan and add one cup of water.
Boil until it will form a ball when dipped in water and
rolled between the thumb and finger. Beat the whites
of the eggs very stiff, and gradually add to them this hot
syrup, stirring all the time. Stir until cold. Mix the rum
and vanilla with the pineapple ice and then beat in the
egg mixture, whip in the champagne and serve immediately.

Quantity:
This will serve twenty-four persons.

*The recipe for pineapple ice you will find elsewhere
in this book.

STRAWBERRY ICE CREAM.

Materials:

1 quart berries.   ½ cup cream.
1½ cups sugar.   1 pint scalded cream.

Way of Preparing:

Mash berries and sprinkle with one cup of sugar. Let stand ½ hour. Strain through coarse cheese cloth, pressing until only the seeds remain. Dissolve ½ cup sugar in the scalded cream and when cooled add to strawberry juice. Turn into freezer. When frozen to mush, add ½ cup plain cream, recover and freeze hard.

Quantity:
This serves six.

TOM AND JERRY.

Materials:

1½ cups milk.   3 cups cream.
1 cup sugar.   3 tablespoonfuls brandy.
6 egg yolks.   2 tablespoonfuls rum.
1 teaspoonful vanilla   1 pinch salt.
   extract.

Way of Preparing:

Make a custard of the milk, sugar, eggs, salt and vanilla, as mentioned in general remarks on ice cream herein. Half freeze, add the rum and brandy and finish freezing.

Quantity:
This will serve eight persons.

VANILLA ICE CREAM.

Materials:

1 pint cream.   1 tablespoonful vanilla ex-
1 pint milk.   tract.
1 lb. sugar.   9 eggs.

Way of Preparing:

Prepare and cook the ingredients as given in the general directions about ice cream, and freeze as directed in "Freezing," also herein.

Quantity:
This will serve six persons.

Invalid Dishes

Such dainties to them, their health it might hurt.
It's like sending them ruffles when wanting a shirt.

—GOLDSMITH.

THE greatest weight is to be attached to the preparation of food for the sick. Oftentimes the diet is of more importance than the drug. Entire wholesomeness of food, the best preparation possible, and prompt and dainty service are necessary requisites.

Do not consult the patient as to the menu, for the various surprises will help to tickle his appetite.

First, prepare the tray with a spotless cloth or napkin folded just to cover; then select the smallest, prettiest dishes from the cupboard, being careful to place everything in an orderly and convenient manner. Serve hot foods on hot dishes, cold food on cold dishes.

For feverish patients, cold water mixed with fruit juices is refreshing and beneficial.

Where raw eggs are ordered, a warm lemonade into which the well-beaten egg is stirred, makes an agreeable change. Care should be taken that the lemonade is not hot enough to cook the egg.

Pillsbury's Best Cereal gruel is most excellent for those needing a food readily assimilated and still full of nourishment. It is non-heat-producing, and therefore valuable for inflammatory and feverish conditions.

ALMOND SOUP.

Materials:

½ lb. almonds.	½ teaspoonful salt.
1 pint milk.	1 pint hot milk.
2 tablespoonfuls sugar.	

Way of Preparing:

Blanch the almonds and pound them in a mortar, gradually adding one pint of milk. When you have pounded it to a smooth paste, and used up all the milk, strain it by squeezing it through a piece of cheesecloth. To the scalded milk add sugar and salt. Now add it to the almond mixture and bring it to the boiling point. Serve hot.

BROILED BEEF JUICE.

2 lbs. lean steak from the top of the round.
Salt, pepper.

Way of Preparing:

Remove any visible fat from the steak, broil over a brisk fire for four minutes, turning it frequently. Cut in pieces about one inch square and gash each piece two or three times. Place in a meat press and squeeze the juice into a hot cup. Season to taste and serve hot.

CHICKEN BROTH.

Materials:

1 4-lb. fowl.   Seasoning.
2 quarts water.

Way of Preparing:

Joint the fowl and skin it, removing all visible fat. Break the bones, place in a saucepan, and pour the water over it. Let stand one hour. Bring it slowly to the boiling point and simmer for three hours. Strain, cool, remove all fat and season to taste. This is served either hot or cold.

BARLEY WATER.

Materials:

2 tablespoonfuls pearl barley.
1 quart water.

Way of Preparing:

Put the barley over the fire in cold water, let it come to a boil and cook five minutes, then drain off the water and rinse the barley in cold water. Then return it to the fire and add one quart of water. Bring it to a boil and simmer until reduced one-half. It may be sweetened and flavored if desired.

OATMEAL GRUEL.

Materials:

½ cup oatmeal.   Sugar.
3 pints boiling water.   Cream.
1 teaspoonful salt.

One of the Pillsbury electric trucks delivering Pillsbury's Best to the city trade

Way of Preparing:

Add the salt to the boiling water, stir in the oatmeal and cook for two and one-half hours in a double boiler. Remove from the fire and strain. When preparing it for a patient, use half a cup of gruel mixed with half a cup of thin cream, two tablespoonfuls of boiling water and sugar to taste.

A pinch of nutmeg or cinnamon is also sometimes added. Other gruels are prepared in the same manner.

CHICKEN CUSTARD.

Materials:

½ cup bread crumbs.   2 tablespoonfuls chopped
2 egg yolks.   breast of chicken.
Pinch of celery salt.   Pinch of salt.
   1 cup milk.

Way of Preparing:

Take the crumbs from the center of a stale loaf and add to them the finely chopped chicken. Beat the yolks until well mixed, and add to them the salt, celery salt and milk. Pour this over the other ingredients, mixing thoroughly. Fill a custard cup with the mixture, place it in a pan of hot water and bake in a moderate oven until set. Serve hot.

FLAXSEED LEMONADE.

Materials:

2 tablespoonfuls flax seed.   Grated rind and juice of three
1 quart boiling water.   lemons.
1 cup sugar.

Way of Preparing:

Blanch the flaxseed, and add the boiling water, let it simmer for three-quarters of an hour, then add the sugar and lemon rind. Let it stand fifteen minutes. Strain and add the lemon juice. Serve either hot or cold. For a bad cough, take a tablespoonful every hour.

Luncheon
Beef Broth   Cocoa Rolls
Chicken Custard   Tea

On endless, inclined belts, the top side running upward, upon which the mustard seed, being round, rolls downward while all other material is carried upward

RICE WATER.

Materials:

2 tablespoonfuls rice. 1 teaspoonful salt.
1 quart boiling water. Flavoring, sugar.

Way of Preparing:

Blanch the rice, drain and add the boiling water. Cook for an hour and a quarter, keeping it simmering only. Then strain, add the salt and use when needed. Sweetening and flavoring to taste may be added if desired. Rice water is also used to dilute milk and is sometimes combined with chicken broth.

SYLLABUB.

Materials:

4 egg yolks. 1 pint milk.
1 tablespoonful flour. ¾ cup sugar.
1 teaspoonful flavoring 1 pint whipped cream.
    extract.

Way of Preparing:

Mix half the sugar with the flour, bring the milk to a boiling point and add sugar and flour to it. Cook in a double boiler ten minutes. Beat the egg yolks and add the other half of the sugar to them. Now add this to the milk mixture, cook five minutes, stirring all the time. Remove from the fire and add the flavoring extract. Let the mixture get cold. When serving fill a tumbler half full of this custard and finish filling with whipped cream.

Note:

Other dishes equally acceptable to invalids are—
Egg Nogg.
Sherry and Egg.
Tenderloin Steak with Beef Juice.
Broiled Squabs.
Junket.
Raw Beef Sandwich.
Broiled Spring Chicken.
Hot Orange or Pineapple Juice served in a cup, etc., etc.

WINE WHEY.

Materials:

1 pint milk. ½ pint sherry wine.

Way of Preparing:

Heat the milk to a boiling point, then add the sherry. Bring it again to the boiling point and strain through cheesecloth.

Meats

*"They that have no other meat,
Bread and butter are glad to eat."*

NEXT to bread, meat forms the principal food on our tables. We not only eat more meat as a nation, but provide other nations with more than anyone else. Beef, veal, mutton and pork are the meats of our households. The vast majority of our housekeepers are not sufficiently well informed as to the proper way of cutting up an animal. Hence they rely entirely too much upon their butchers in the purchase of their meats. It must be assumed that the readers of these recipes are measurably familiar with that part of the knowledge required to be a good buyer of meat at retail. If not, there are more extensive works on cooking for acquiring it.

The cheaper parts of a first-class animal may be prepared to furnish far better dishes than the high-priced portions of an inferior animal; in other words, a stew from the fore-quarter of a first-class animal will be better than a roast from the loin of an inferior animal, and it will be cheaper.

BAKED LIVER LARDED.

Materials:

1 calf's liver.	2 cups boiling water.
½ lb. fat salt pork.	2 tablespoonfuls butter.
1 carrot.	2 tablespoonfuls flour.
1 onion.	½ teaspoonful salt.
1 red pepper.	Juice of 1 lemon.
½ bayleaf.	

Way of Preparing:

Skewer the liver into shape and lard it with strips of the fat pork. Surround it with the vegetables chopped fine. Add to the boiling water the seasoning, and pour this over the liver. Cover and bake for one hour and a half. Uncover and bake fifteen minutes longer. Remove from the pan, add the lemon juice to the liquor, strain over the liver and serve.

Quantity:

This will serve four persons.

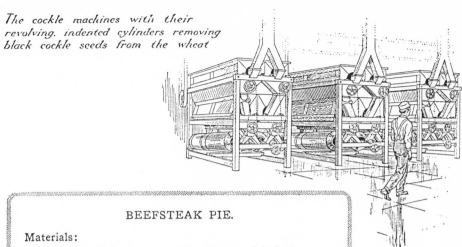

The cockle machines with their revolving, indented cylinders removing black cockle seeds from the wheat

BEEFSTEAK PIE.

Materials:

2 lbs. round steak,
  ½-inch thick.
1 onion sliced.
1 heaping tablespoonful flour.
2 tablespoonfuls butter.
2 medium potatoes, sliced thin.
1 teaspoonful salt.
½ teaspoonful pepper.

Way of Preparing:

Cut the steak into strips one and one-half inch long and one inch wide, place the strips in a saucepan, cover with boiling water, add the sliced onion, and simmer until the meat is tender. Remove the meat, discard the onion, add the potatoes to the liquor and parboil six minutes. Then remove the potatoes. Now measure the liquor and add enough boiling water to make one pint and add the seasonings. Cream the butter and flour together, add it to the liquor and cook five minutes. In the bottom of a pudding dish, place a layer of one-half the parboiled potatoes and on top of this layer arrange the meat, placing the other half of the potatoes in a layer on top of it. Pour over this sufficient gravy to entirely cover the contents of the baking dish. Now let it cool; when cool, cover it with a crust and bake in a hot oven.

The crust is made as follows:

Materials:

1 cup flour.
1 rounding tablespoonful butter.
1 rounding tablespoonful lard.
½ teaspoonful salt.
1 teaspoonful baking powder.
Milk.

Way of Preparing:

Sift the flour, baking powder and salt, cream the butter and lard together and combine them with the dry ingredients, mixing them thoroughly with your finger tips. Now add enough milk to make a soft dough, roll it out about one-quarter of an inch thick, and cover with it the contents of your pudding dish.

Quantity:

This will serve six persons.

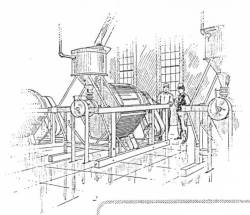

Wheat washers that immerse and agitate the wheat in running water until it is absolutely clean

BEEF LOAF.

Materials:

3 lbs. lean beef.	1 teaspoonful salt.
½ lb. raw ham.	1 teaspoonful pepper.
3 eggs, well beaten.	3 tablespoonfuls cream.
3 soda crackers, rolled fine.	6 hard boiled eggs.

Way of Preparing:

Chop the beef and ham very fine and then add the salt and pepper, the cracker crumbs, the well beaten eggs, and the cream. Mix all these together perfectly, grease a breadpan thoroughly, and press half the mixture into it firmly. Trim each end of your hard boiled eggs so as to make a flat surface, then put them on top of the mixture in the breadpan, placing them in a row end to end. Now pack on top the balance of your meat, pressing it down firmly. Cover and bake in a moderate oven one hour. Uncover and bake half an hour longer. Serve either hot or cold in slices.

Quantity:

This will serve ten persons.

BEEF TONGUE PIQUANT.

Materials:

1 fresh tongue.	1 onion.
1 carrot.	1 stalk celery.
1 red pepper.	1 teaspoonful salt.

Way of Preparing:

Place the tongue in a kettle and cover with boiling water, adding the vegetables and seasoning. Cover and cook until tender. Take the tongue from the kettle and remove the skin and root. Put back into the kettle and reheat. Serve it sliced into half-inch slices accompanied by a

SAUCE

made of the following:

Materials:

4 tablespoonfuls of flour.	2 tablespoonfuls butter.
¾ cup brown stock.	1 teaspoonful salt.
½ teaspoonful paprika.	2 tablespoonfuls lemon-juice.
1 cucumber pickle, chopped.	1 tablespoonful seeded raisins.

Way of Preparing:

Brown the flour in the butter, then add the stock and cook five minutes. Season with the salt, paprika, lemon-juice, cucumber pickle, chopped fine, and the seeded raisins. Mix thoroughly and serve hot.

CALVES' TONGUE.

Materials:

4 calves' tongues.	2 cups boiling water.
1 onion.	1 tablespoonful vinegar.
1 teaspoonful salt.	½ teaspoonful salt.
½ teaspoonful pepper.	¼ teaspoonful paprika.
3 tablespoonfuls flour.	1 tablespoonful capers.
3 tablespoonfuls butter.	12 stoned olives sliced.

Way of Preparing:

Cover the tongues with boiling water, and add the onion, sliced together with one teaspoonful of salt and one-half teaspoonful of pepper. Cover and simmer slowly until thoroughly done. Remove from the water and skin the tongues, and cut them lengthwise in halves. Brown the butter in a saucepan, add the flour and brown thoroughly, stirring carefully all the while, and then add the boiling water. Season with the other one-half teaspoonful of salt, paprika, vinegar and capers. Then add the tongues, which should have been reheated. Dish on a hot platter, add the olives and serve.

Quantity:

This will serve four persons.

CORN BEEF HASH.

Materials:

1 pint chopped cold corned beef.	1 pint cold chopped potatoes.
½ teaspoonful salt.	½ teaspoonful pepper.
¼ cup cream.	1 tablespoonful butter.
	Onion.

Way of Preparing:

Rub the inside of your frying pan with a cut onion. Put in the butter and let it get hot. Then add the meat, potatoes, salt and pepper, having them well mixed. Moisten the whole with the cream, spread evenly and place the pan so that the hash can brown slowly and evenly underneath. When done, fold over and turn out on the platter. You can do the browning in the oven if you prefer.

Wheat dryers forcing hot air through the washed wheat and drying it sufficiently for proper milling

Quantity:

This will serve four persons.

CREOLE TRIPE.

Materials:

2 pints tripe.	½ cup drained tomatoes.
2 tablespoonfuls butter.	3 fresh mushrooms.
1 onion.	1 teaspoonful salt.
½ green pepper.	Boiled rice.
1 tablespoonful flour.	Parsley chopped.
1 cup boiling water.	

Way of Preparing:

Put the butter in a saucepan and cook in it the onion, chopped fine. Then add the flour, the green pepper, finely chopped, the boiling water, the tomatoes, the mushrooms, peeled and sliced and the salt, boil five minutes. Cut the tripe in pieces one and one-half inch square, and press them between folds of cheese cloth, to remove all the moisture. Add the tripe to the contents of the saucepan, and simmer ten minutes. Dish on a hot platter, surrounded by a border of boiled rice. Sprinkle with finely chopped parsley and serve.

Quantity:

This will serve five persons.

CURRIED LAMB.

Materials:

4 cups lamb, cut in inch pieces.	3 sprigs parsley.
1 large onion sliced.	2 tablespoonfuls butter.
1 quart boiling water.	2 tablespoonfuls flour.
1 stalk celery.	1 teaspoonful curry powder.
3 sprigs thyme.	1 teaspoonful salt.
½ teaspoonful pepper.	Cold water.
	Boiled rice.

Way of Preparing:

Put the lamb in a kettle, cover with cold water, and bring to the boiling point. Pour off the water and rinse the meat in cold water, return it to the kettle and add one quart of boiling water, the onion cut in slices, the thyme and the parsley. Simmer slowly until the meat is tender, then remove it and strain the liquor. Melt the butter in a saucepan and add the flour, then add the curry powder, salt, pepper and strained liquor. Cook three minutes, add the meat; thoroughly reheat and serve with a garniture of boiled rice.

Dinner

Beef Steak Pie

Baked Potatoes   Egg Plant

Wheat Bread   Cherry Salad

Cocoa

The scourers remove impurities and the hairy fuzz found on one end of each kernel of wheat

Quantity:

This will serve six persons.

DEVILED STEAK.

Materials:

1 flank steak.	½ teaspoonful pepper.
1 large onion.	⅛ teaspoonful paprika.
2 tablespoonfuls butter.	1 teaspoonful mustard.
2 tablespoonfuls flour.	3 tablespoonfuls vinegar.
1 teaspoonful salt.	2 cups hot water.

Way of Preparing:

Melt the butter in a frying pan, slice the onion and fry it in the butter. Remove the onion when it is brown. Cut the steak in pieces three inches long and two inches wide, dredge them lightly in flour and fry in the butter. Remove the meat from the frying pan and add to the butter the salt, vinegar, mustard, pepper, paprika and the remaining flour. Then add the hot water. Replace the steak in the frying pan, cover closely and allow it to simmer until the steak is tender. Dish on a hot platter, pour the gravy over it, garnish with fried potatoes and serve.

Quantity:

This will serve six persons.

FRIED PIGS' FEET.

Materials:

Pigs' feet.	Lard and butter.
Lemon juice.	Batter to taste.
Salt and pepper.	

Way of Preparing:

Wash the feet and put them on to boil in cold water. Bring them quickly to the boiling point and then reduce the heat. Allow them to simmer until very tender, then remove them from the kettle, and allow them to get cold. When cold and firm, split them in halves with a sharp knife, season with pepper and salt, dip them in batter and fry in deep fat. Drain on blotting paper and serve very hot. Instead of frying them you may make—

BROILED PIGS' FEET.

by sprinkling them with pepper and salt and broiling them for ten minutes. Dress with butter and lemon juice.

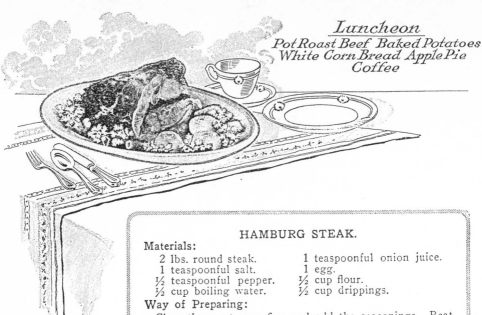

HAMBURG STEAK.

Materials:

2 lbs. round steak.	1 teaspoonful onion juice.
1 teaspoonful salt.	1 egg.
½ teaspoonful pepper.	½ cup flour.
½ cup boiling water.	½ cup drippings.

Way of Preparing:

Chop the meat very fine and add the seasonings. Beat the egg, and mix with the meat. Divide into four equal portions, and shape into round cakes, about one inch thick. Dredge these on both sides with flour, and fry in the drippings, turning them so as to brown both sides. When nicely browned, add the half-cup of boiling water. Cover closely and simmer for forty-five minutes.

Quantity:

This will serve four persons.

HUNGARIAN GOULASH.

A National Dish ("Gulyas" in Hungarian).

Materials:

3 lbs. veal in in. cubes.	½ teaspoonful paprika.
3 large potatoes diced.	1 cup butter or drippings.
½ cup water.	1 cup cream.
1 teaspoonful salt.	½ teaspoonful black pepper.
3 large onions, sliced.	

Way of Preparing:

Put the butter or drippings in a kettle on the range, and when hot add the onions and fry them; add the veal and cook until brown. Add the water, cover closely, and cook very slowly until the meat is tender, then add the seasonings and place the potatoes on top of the meat. Cover and cook until the potatoes are tender, but not falling to pieces. Then add the cream and cook five minutes longer.

Quantity:

This dish will serve six persons.

PORK TENDERLOIN LARDED.

Materials:

½ lb. fat pork.	2 tablespoonfuls butter.
4 large pork tender-	1 teaspoonful salt.
loins.	½ teaspoonful pepper.
1 cup cracker crumbs.	1 teaspoonful poultry sea-
1 cup boiling water.	soning.

Way of Preparing:

Wipe the tenderloins clean with a damp cloth. With a sharp knife make a deep pocket lengthwise in each tenderloin, laying the tenderloin flat on the table and making the incisions along the sides. Cut your pork into long thin strips, and with a larding needle lard each tenderloin. Melt the butter in the water, add the seasonings and the cracker crumbs, combining all thoroughly. Now fill each pocket in the tenderloins with this stuffing, sew up the pockets closely with a coarse thread and needle, place the tenderloins in a baking pan, and bake in a brisk oven forty-five minutes, basting constantly with a

BROWN SAUCE

made of the following:

Materials:

2 tablespoonfuls butter.   ½ teaspoonful salt.
1 small onion.   ¼ teaspoonful pepper.
2 tablespoonfuls flour.   ½ bayleaf.
1½ cups boiling water.

Way of Preparing:

Cook the onion in the butter five minutes. Remove the onion, add the flour, and stir until well browned. Add the seasonings and the boiling water. Keep hot and baste your tenderloins with it. When the tenderloins are done, serve them on a hot platter and pour around them any remaining sauce.

Quantity:

This will serve eight persons.

POT ROAST BEEF.

Materials:

5 lbs. beef.   1 carrot, chopped fine.
½ lb. suet.   1 tablespoonful flour.
6 cloves.   1 pint boiling water.
2 bayleaves.   Salt and pepper.
2 slices onion.

Heaters and steamers that temper the wheat as it passes on to be ground

Way of Preparing:

Put the suet in a kettle and add the onions, bay-leaves, cloves and chopped carrot; let it cook five minutes and get very hot. Put in the meat, well seasoned with salt and pepper and brown it on both sides. Add the water, cover closely and simmer until very tender. Remove from the pot and thicken the liquor remaining in the pot with the flour. Strain and serve it in a sauceboat.

Note.—As the roast cooks, add boiling water to keep the quantity the same as at first.

Quantity:

This will serve eight persons.

SPANISH HASH.

Materials:

1 cup cold roast meat (any kind).	Tabasco sauce, pepper and salt.
4 cold boiled potatoes.	1 green pepper.
2 small onions.	1 egg.
	1 cup tomatoes, canned.

Way of Preparing:

Chop together your cold potatoes, onions and green pepper, then add one cup chopped cold roast meat and one of tomatoes. Season with pepper and salt, and three drops of tabasco sauce; then add the egg, well beaten. Drop by spoonfuls into your muffin-rings. Bake in a hot oven and serve with tomato sauce.

ESCALLOPED BRAINS.

Materials:

Calves' brains.	Salt and pepper.
Bread crumbs.	Butter.
Milk.	

Way of Preparing:

Soak the brains in cold water one hour. Parboil in salted water ten minutes. Remove the skins. Grease a baking dish and put in a layer of the brains, sliced. Then put on a layer of crumbs, sprinkle with salt and pepper and dot with butter. Now add another layer of brains, then another one of crumbs, salt and pepper and butter, alternating in this way until the dish is nearly full. Fill with milk and bake three-quarters of an hour in a moderate oven.

Dinner
Cream of Celery Soup
Veal Loaf   Rice   Boiled Potatoes
Potatoe Bread   Apple Pie
Coffee

The grinding floor with its long rows of roller mills that grind the whole day long

STUFFED HAM.

Materials:

1 medium sized ham.
1 pint bread crumbs.
1 teaspoonful mustard.
3 eggs, well beaten.
1 teaspoonful red pepper.
1 cup brown sugar.
3 pickles, chopped.
1 teaspoonful cloves.

1 teaspoonful allspice.
1 teaspoonful cinnamon.
1 teaspoonful black pepper.
1 tablespoonful chopped celery.
1 cup sweet milk.
Boiled eggs.
Cloves.

Way of Preparing:

Boil the ham for three hours; after it is cold, skin it and make incisions in the ham, one inch apart from each other, lengthwise, and as deep as possible.

Make a stuffing of the bread crumbs and a teaspoonful each of mustard, cloves, cinnamon, allspice, three well-beaten eggs, black and red pepper mixed, the chopped celery, brown sugar, the chopped pickles and the sweet milk. Mix these ingredients thoroughly into a soft paste, fill the incisions and cover the ham with the same.

Put in the oven and brown slowly. Garnish the ham, when done, with slices of boiled egg and pickles, sticking a whole clove into each piece of pickle.

VEAL LOAF.

Materials:

3 lbs. lean veal.
½ lb. raw ham.
3 eggs, well beaten.
3 soda crackers, rolled fine.

1 teaspoonful salt.
1 teaspoonful pepper.
3 tablespoonfuls cream.
2 tablespoonfuls boiling water.

Way of Preparing:

Chop the veal and ham very fine, then add the salt and pepper, the cracker crumbs, the well beaten eggs, the cream and the hot water. Mix all these together very thoroughly, grease a bread-pan perfectly and pack the mixture into it, pressing it down firmly. Cover and bake in a moderate oven one hour. Uncover and bake half an hour longer. Serve either hot or cold in slices.

Quantity:

This will serve eight persons.

Corrugated Rolls of the steel grinding mills

PIES AND PASTRY.

PIES are one of the few specifically national American dishes. The digestibility of pies has been called into question. Properly made pies are as digestible as anything else.

Paste for pies should be quite thin and rolled a little larger than the tin to allow for shrinkage. Allow more paste for the upper than the under crust, and be sure to perforate the former. Always brush the under crust with cold water and press the upper one down on it. When baking a juicy fruit pie make an incision in the center and place a small funnel-shaped piece of paper into the incision. This will keep the juice from escaping at the sides of the pie. Never grease a pie tin. Properly made pastry will grease its own tin. For baking, pastry requires from thirty to forty-five minutes.

APPLE PIE.

Materials:

Apples.	Pie Paste.
Sugar.	Cinnamon.
Water.	Butter.

Way of Preparing:

Line a deep pie tin with rich paste, select large tart apples. Pare and quarter and cut each quarter into four pieces. Put an even layer of these pieces in the prepared tin, sprinkle with sugar, dot with butter, dust with cinnamon and bake in a moderate oven for forty-five minutes.

Three tablespoons of prepared tea are sometimes used instead of the water for moistening.

Quantity:

This will serve four or six.

CHERRY PIE.

Materials:

1 quart cherries.	1 tablespoonful flour.
1 cup sugar.	Pastry.

PIES AND PASTRY.

Way of Preparing:
Stem and pit the cherries, sift the flour and sugar together and add to the cherries. Line a pie tin with rich pastry. Put in the prepared cherries, cover with pastry, and bake in a moderate oven for thirty-five minutes.

Quantity:
Serve four or six persons.

CHEESE PIE.

Materials:

4 eggs.	1 lemon.
1 lb. cottage cheese.	1½ cups sugar.

Way of Preparing:
Beat the whites and yolks of the eggs separately. To the beaten yolks add the sugar, beating thoroughly, then add the grated rind and the juice of the lemon. Pass the cheese through a colander, and then add it, beating again thoroughly. Lastly, stir in the beaten whites. Line a pie tin with a raw pie crust, pour in the mixture and bake in a moderate oven.

Quantity:
This will serve four or six persons.

CREAM PUFFS.

Materials:

1 cup flour.	½ lb. butter.
¾ cup water.	5 eggs.
Pinch salt.	Filling.

Way of Preparing:
Heat the water and add the butter and salt. When this boils, stir in the flour. Take care to have no lumps. Cook until the mixture leaves the side of the saucepan. Pour out and allow it to cool. When nearly cold add the unbeaten eggs, one at a time. Mix in each one thoroughly before adding the next. After adding all, cover the mixture and let it stand for one hour. When ready to bake, drop it by the spoonful on buttered tins, leaving space for them to rise. Bake in a moderate oven for forty-five minutes. They should feel dry and crisp to the touch. When cold, split and fill with whipped cream. If desired, they can be fried in deep fat, like doughnuts. If you intend frying them, use only a teaspoonful at a time.

Quantity:
Makes eighteen Cream Puffs.

The old, reliable mill-stones, tho immortalized in story, are fast giving way to the steel roller mill

CUSTARD PIE.

Materials:

4 eggs.
1 pint sweet milk.
1 heaping tablespoonful flour.

4 heaping tablespoonfuls sugar.
Flavoring extract.

Way of Preparing:

Beat the eggs just enough to blend thoroughly, then add the sugar, then the flour, and lastly the milk.

Flavor to taste and bake in a raw crust until the custard is set.

Quantity:

This will serve four or six persons.

DULING APPLE DUMPLING.

Materials:

2 cups flour.
2 teaspoonfuls baking powder.
1 teaspoonful salt.
1 tablespoonful butter.
1 tablespoonful lard.

$\frac{7}{8}$ cup sweet milk.
1 teaspoonful cinnamon.
2 tablespoonfuls brown sugar.
3 tart apples, chopped.

Way of Preparing:

Sift the flour, baking powder and salt. Work into these the butter and lard. Then make a dough, using the milk. Place on your molding board. Roll out into a sheet one-half an inch thick. Brush with melted butter and sprinkle with the brown sugar and cinnamon. Then cover with the chopped apples. Roll it up, as you would a jelly roll, and cut into twelve equal slices. Place the slices on end in a buttered pan. Pour over them the sauce and bake in a brisk oven for twenty-five minutes. Following is the

DUMPLING SAUCE.

Materials:

1 cup sugar.
1 tablespoonful butter.
1 tablespoonful flour.

$\frac{1}{2}$ teaspoonful salt.
1 cup hot water.
$\frac{1}{2}$ lemon, sliced.

Way of Preparing:

Mix the sugar, flour and salt. Add butter, sliced lemon and hot water. Stir until well mixed. Cook three minutes, and then pour it over the raw dumplings.

Quantity:

This will serve twelve people.

GRANDMOTHER'S PIE.

Materials:
5 eggs.
1 cup sugar.

The grated rind and juice of
two lemons.
Pastry.

Way of Preparing:
Beat the eggs, add the sugar, then the rind and juice
of the lemons. Bake in a small tart-pan, lined with rich
crust.

Quantity:
This will serve four persons.

LEMON CREAM PIE.

Materials:
4 eggs.
1 cup sugar.
2 heaping tablespoonfuls
flour.

1½ cups boiling water.
The grated rind and juice of
two lemons.

Way of Preparing:
Beat the yolks and whites of the eggs separately. To
the beaten yolks add the sugar, flour, lemon juice and
rind, and lastly the boiling water; cook in a double boiler
and when it begins to thicken, add to it one-half of
rind, and lastly the boiling water; cook in a double boiler
and when it begins to thicken, add to it one-half of the
beaten whites. Stir this in thoroughly and let it cook
until it is as thick as desired.

Use the remainder of the whites for the meringue on
top of the pie. After your custard has cooled, fill a baked
shell, pile the meringue on top, and bake in a very slow
oven until the meringue is brown.

Quantity:
This will serve four or six persons.

MINCE PIE.

Materials:
4 lbs. beef tenderloin or
tongue.
3 lbs. suet.
3 lbs. brown sugar.
3 lbs. seeded raisins.
3 lbs. currants.
1 oz. mace.
1 oz. nutmeg.
1 oz. cinnamon.
1 oz. cloves.

10 large apples, chopped fine.
2 lbs. citron, sliced.
Grated rind and juice of four
lemons.
Juice and grated rind of four
oranges.
1 quart brandy.
1 pint Madeira wine.
1 tablespoonful salt.

Bolting the flour in silk covered reels through which the flour is directed and sifted out as they revolve

Way of Preparing:

Boil the beef very well done, and chop it fine. Chop suet and apples and add to the beef. Mix the sugar, mace, nutmeg, cinnamon and cloves, and add to them the wine, brandy, lemon juice and orange juice.

Mix the raisins, currants, citron and lemon and orange rinds.

Now combine gradually the three sets of ingredients. after having added the salt to the liquid part, using a portion of each until all are used.

Pack in stone jars, cover closely and keep in a dry cool closet.

Quantity:

This will make enough to last all winter.

PIE CRUST.

Materials:

1 cup Pillsbury's Best.
3 level tablespoons shortening (equal parts of butter and lard or lard only).
¼ teaspoon baking powder.
½ teaspoon salt.

Preparation:

Mix together with a knife, using sufficient ice cold water to make a fairly soft dough (about ¼ cupful). Roll out thin into two crusts, keeping everything as cold as possible. If desired, sufficient may be made at one time to last several days, but it must be kept ice cold.

Note:

The use of milk instead of water makes much finer pastry.

PUMPKIN PIE.

Materials:

3 eggs.
1 cup sugar.
1 cup stewed pumpkin.
1 teaspoonful ginger.

1 teaspoonful cinnamon.
½ teaspoonful allspice.
½ teaspoonful cloves.
1 pint milk.

Way of Preparing:

Beat the eggs, add to them the sugar, the pumpkin and the spices. Beat it thoroughly and then add the milk and mix thoroughly, then bake in a raw crust.

Quantity:

This will serve four or six persons.

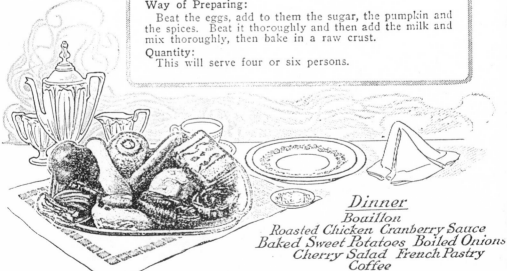

Dinner
Bouillon
Roasted Chicken Cranberry Sauce
Baked Sweet Potatoes Boiled Onions
Cherry Salad French Pastry
Coffee

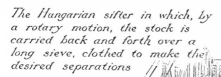

The Hungarian sifter in which, by a rotary motion, the stock is carried back and forth over a long sieve, clothed to make the desired separations

SQUASH PIE No. 1.

Materials:

2 cups prepared squash.	1 cup milk.
½ cup sugar.	½ teaspoonful cinnamon.
2 eggs.	½ teaspoonful ginger.
1 tablespoonful flour.	¼ teaspoonful salt.

Way of Preparing:

Beat the eggs and add the sugar, then the squash, salt and spices. After that add the flour and lastly, add the milk gradually. Line a pie plate with pastry and pour on it the mixture. Bake for five minutes in a brisk oven.

Reduce the heat and bake slowly until the custard is set.

You can make a

SWEET POTATO PIE.

in precisely the same way, substituting sweet potatoes in the place of squash.

Quantity:

This will serve four or six persons.

SQUASH PIE No. 2.

Materials:

1½ cups squash.	½ teaspoonful salt.
⅓ cup sugar.	¼ teaspoonful nutmeg.
1 egg.	¼ teaspoonful cinnamon.
1 cup milk.	1 tablespoonful melted butter.

Way of Preparing:

Steam and strain squash to make 1½ cups. Add sugar, salt, spice, butter, egg slightly beaten, and milk gradually.

After the crust is set, bake slowly.

If a richer pie is desired, omit butter, take new milk, or half milk and half cream, and use one more egg yolk.

Quantity:

This makes one large pie.

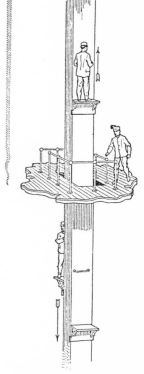

Belt elevator, used by the millers, running continuously up and down through the mills

85

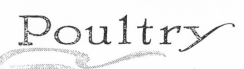

Poultry

"A good fire makes a good cook"

CHICKEN CROQUETTES.

Materials:

1 pint cold cooked chicken.	1 teaspoonful onion juice.
½ pint milk.	1 teaspoonful salt.
1 heaping tablespoonful butter.	¼ teaspoonful nutmeg.
	½ teaspoonful pepper.
2 tablespoonfuls flour.	Flour, beaten eggs, cracker crumbs, lard.

Way of Preparing:

Chop the meat very fine. Heat the milk in a double boiler. Cream the butter, and flour, and add it to the milk, then add the onion juice and seasonings. Cook until you have a thick sauce. Pour this over the chopped chicken, and mix thoroughly, then let it cool, and form into shapes. Flour lightly, dip shapes into the beaten eggs, roll in cracker crumbs, and fry in deep fat.

Quantity:

This will serve six persons.

CHICKEN EN CASSEROLE.

(Casserole is the French for an earthen, covered dish.)

Materials:

2½ lbs. chicken.	1 teaspoonful salt.
1 can mushrooms.	½ teaspoonful pepper.
1 carrot.	1 tablespoonful flour.
1 onion.	2 cups boiling water.
1 tablespoonful chopped parsley.	1 stalk celery.
	½ cup of butter.

Way of Preparing:

Clean and dress the chicken and steam it until tender. Melt the butter in a frying pan, add all the vegetables, chopped fine, cook five minutes and then add the flour. Add all the seasonings to the hot water, pour it into the frying pan and let it cook five minutes. Put the chicken in a casserole, dredge with flour, dust with salt and pepper, and pour the contents of the frying pan over it. Place it in the oven and cook until the chicken is thoroughly browned. Remove from the oven, cover the dish and serve in the casserole.

Quantity:

This will serve five persons.

FRIED SPRING CHICKEN.
Southern Style.

Materials:

1 chicken.	1 cup lard.
½ cup flour.	Pepper and salt.

Way of Preparing:

Select a large, plump spring chicken, kill, scald and pluck. Draw, and cut into the natural joints. Then put them into icewater for five minutes. Drain and place on a platter in the ice box for two hours. Dredge thickly with flour and sprinkle with salt and pepper. Place the lard in a frying pan and when it is hot saute the chicken in it, taking care to turn it often so it will not burn, but cook thoroughly, serve with cream gravy.

Some prefer frying bacon enough with the chicken to make the required amount of fat. If you do so, serve some of the bacon with the chicken.

POTATO STUFFING.
For Fowl.

Materials:

2 cups hot, mashed potatoes.	1 teaspoonful onion juice.
	¼ cup butter.
1 cup crumbs.	1 teaspoonful salt.
¼ cup salt pork, chopped.	½ teaspoonful sage.
	1 egg.

Way of Preparing:

Add to the potatoes the butter, egg, salt, onion juice, sage, crumbs, and pork, mix thoroughly and use as stuffing.

ROAST GOOSE.

Materials:

1 large goose.	Pepper.
6 strips salt pork.	Stuffing.
1 cup water.	Apple sauce.
Salt.	Watercress.

Way of Preparing:

Scrub the goose with hot soap suds, then draw, wash thoroughly in cold water and wipe dry. Stuff, truss, sprinkle with salt and pepper and cover the entire breast with strips of salt pork. Place on the rack in the dripping pan, pour the water into the latter under the goose. Place in a hot oven and bake for two hours and a half, basting every ten minutes. Remove the pork the last half hour. Garnish the dish with watercress and serve with apple sauce.

The recipe for stuffing made of potatoes is given herein.

The modern sifting machine through which, by a gentle rotary motion, the stock is carried down over numerous small sieves arranged to make the necessary separations

SPANISH STEW.

Materials:

3½ lbs. chicken.
5 ripe tomatoes.
4 red peppers.
1 can French peas.
1 can mushrooms.
3 large potatoes.

1 teaspoonful salt.
1 quart boiling water.
1 onion.
Boiled rice or mashed potatoes.

Way of Preparing:

Clean and joint the chicken, slice the tomatoes, shred the peppers (removing seeds) and slice the onions. Place the chicken in a kettle with the tomatoes, peppers and onions. Add the boiling water. Cover the kettle and simmer until the chicken is tender, then remove the chicken, strain what remains in the kettle and rub the vegetable part through a sieve. Return vegetables to the kettle and add one can of French peas, a can of mushrooms and the potatoes, grated, also the salt and cook until the potatoes are tender. Then replace the chicken in the kettle and heat thoroughly.

Serve with a border of mashed potatoes or boiled rice.

Quantity:

This will serve eight persons.

STEWED DUCK.

Materials:

Several slices of lean, cold boiled ham, or salt pork (minced fine.)
1 large onion (chopped.)
½ teaspoonful powdered sage.

½ teaspoonful parsley.
½ teaspoonful brown sugar
½ teaspoonful catsup.
1 tablespoonful browned flour, some black pepper.

Way of Preparing:

Clean and divide as for fricasse. Put in a sauce pan with several slices of lean, cold boiled ham or salt pork, minced fine. Stew slowly, closely covered, for one hour. Then stir in one large onion (chopped), one-half teaspoonful powdered sage, same amount of parsley, one tablespoonful of catsup, some black pepper. Stew until tender, then add one teaspoonful of brown sugar, one tablespoonful of browned flour, mixed with cold water. Boil up once and serve in dish. Serve with green peas.

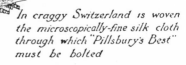

In craggy Switzerland is woven the microscopically-fine silk cloth through which "Pillsbury's Best" must be bolted

TURKEY TIMBALES.

Materials:

½ lb. boneless turkey.
1 gill of thin cream.
3 whites of eggs (un-
   beaten.)
1 saltspoon of salt.

1 dash cayenne pepper.
1 tablespoonful chopped
   mushrooms.
½ teaspoonful onion juice.
1 tablespoonful Worcestershire sauce.

Way of Preparing:

Take one-half pound of boneless turkey. Chop and pound to a paste; add gradually one gill of thin cream; then add, one at a time, the whites of three eggs (unbeaten), carefully beating one in before the next is added. Add one saltspoonful of salt, a dash of cayenne pepper and one tablespoonful of finely chopped mushrooms, half a teaspoonful of onion juice, and one tablespoonful of Worcestershire sauce. Then fold in the stiffly beaten whites of two eggs. Fill well buttered timbale cups half full of the mixture; stand them in a pan of hot water; bake twenty minutes in moderate oven. Serve hot with mushroom sauce.

TURKEY, ESCALLOPED.

Materials:

2 eggs (beaten).
2 tablespoonful (milk).
Butter.

Salt.
Pepper.
Rolled cracked crumbs.

Way of Preparing:

Butter a deep dish and line it with cracker crumbs. In the bottom put a layer of crumbs, seasoned with butter, pepper and salt, then a layer of cold turkey chopped fine. Continue in this way until the dish is full, adding the stuffing and gravy of the turkey. Beat two eggs and add to them two tablespoonsful of milk, butter, salt, pepper and rolled cracker crumbs. Spread this thickly over the top of the turkey and bake for half an hour. Keep it covered the first twenty minutes, then remove the cover and brown.

Puddings

The proof of the pudding is the eating
—CERVANTES

BREAD PUDDING.

Materials:

1 pint bread crumbs.	3 eggs.
3 cups milk.	1 teaspoonful vanilla.
½ cup sugar.	½ teaspoonful salt.
¼ cup butter.	1 cup chopped citron.

Way of Preparing:

Heat the milk and pour over the crumbs. Cream the butter and sugar and add the eggs, salt and vanilla. When the milk is cold combine the two mixtures and add the chopped citron. Pour into a buttered pudding dish and bake forty minutes. Serve with any desired sauce.

Quantity:

This will serve six persons.

FROZEN PUDDING.

Materials:

1 pint milk.	1 lb. French candied fruits
Scant ½ cup flour.	(½ lb. will do).
2 tablespoonfuls gelatine.	2 eggs.
2 cups sugar.	1 quart cream.
	4 tablespoonfuls wine.

Way of Preparing:

Let the milk come to a boil. Beat the flour, one cup of sugar and the eggs together and stir into the boiling milk. Cook 20 minutes and then add your gelatine after soaking one or two hours. Set away to cool. When cool, add the wine, one cup of sugar and the cream. Freeze ten minutes, then add the fruit and finish freezing. Take out the beater, pack smoothly and set away for an hour or two.

Quantity:

This will serve six or eight persons.

HOT SNOW BALLS.

Materials:

3 cups pastry flour.	½ cup milk.
1 cup confectioners'	Whites of 6 eggs.
XXXX sugar.	3 teaspoonfuls baking pow-
½ cup butter.	der.

Way of Preparing:

Cream the butter and add the sugar. Beat for five minutes. Sift the flour and baking powder and add to the former, alternating with the milk. Lastly fold in the stiffly-beaten whites of the eggs. Fill buttered cups half full and steam for thirty minutes. Serve with orange marmalade and whipped cream or with your favorite sauce.

Quantity:

This will serve twelve persons.

MACAROON PUDDING.

Materials:

½ lbs. macaroons.	Sherry wine.
2 eggs.	5 tablespoonfuls sugar.
¼ teaspoonful salt.	1 cup milk.
1 cup cream.	2 tablespoonfuls almonds,
¼ teaspoonful almond	blanched and chopped.
extract.	

Way of Preparing:

Soak a dozen macaroons ten minutes in sherry wine and then remove them. Beat two eggs slightly and add the sugar, salt, milk and the cream, then add the chopped almonds, the almond extract and four finely-powdered macaroons. Turn this mixture into a pudding dish, arrange your soaked macaroons on top, cover and bake thirty minutes in a hot oven.

Quantity:

This will serve six persons.

PINEAPPLE PUDDING.

Materials:

1 can pineapple.	½ box gelatine, or 2½ table-
1 small tea cup sugar.	spoonfuls granulated gel-
½ pint whipped cream.	atine.

Way of Preparing:

Pour juice off of pineapple. Dissolve gelatine in half a pint of hot water. Chop pineapple very fine and mix with sugar. Add this to the dissolved gelatine. When this begins to stiffen, stir in the whipped cream, beating thoroughly.

Set in a cool place to harden.

Quantity:

Will serve six.

Samples representing each days milling of Pillsbury's Best are kept for one year for reference

PLUM PUDDING.

Materials:

½ lb. bread crumbs.
½ lb. suet, chopped.
½ lb. sugar.
4 eggs.
½ lb. seeded raisins.
½ lb. currants.
½ lb. figs, chopped.
1 cup milk.

¼ lb. citron, sliced.
½ cup brandy.
1 teaspoonful nutmeg.
½ teaspoonful cinnamon.
½ teaspoonful cloves.
¼ teaspoonful mace.
1 teaspoonful salt.

Way of Preparing:

Scald the milk and pour it over the crumbs, cream the suet, and add the sugar and the well-beaten yolks of the eggs. When milk and crumbs are cool, combine them with the other mixture, and add the raisins, figs, currants, citron, salt and spices.

Then add the brandy, and lastly, the stiffly-beaten whites of the eggs. Pour into a buttered mold and steam five hours, serve with hard sauce or brandy sauce.

Quantity:

This will make one large or two small puddings.

RICE PUDDING.

Materials:

2 cups boiled rice.
1 pint milk.
4 eggs.
¾ cup sugar.

1 tablespoonful flour.
1 teaspoonful lemon extract.

Way of Preparing:

Slightly beat the eggs. Add the sugar and flour and mix with the rice. Then add the flavoring and lastly the milk. Bake in a moderate oven until set. Serve with whipped cream or sauce.

This can be made very rich by spreading on top a layer of orange marmalade and covering it with a meringue.

Quantity:

This will serve six persons.

RUSSIAN CREAM.

Materials:

⅓ box gelatine.
1 pint milk.
1 teaspoonful vanilla.

4 eggs.
½ cup sugar.
Hot water.

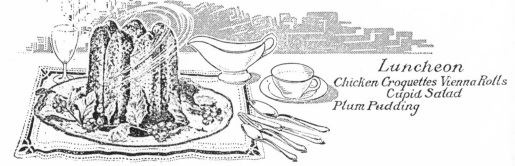

Luncheon
Chicken Croquettes Vienna Rolls
Cupid Salad
Plum Pudding

Way of Preparing:

Dissolve the gelatine in hot water. Beat the yolks of the eggs separately with the sugar. Stir in the milk and make into a custard in a double boiler. Before removing from the range stir in the dissolved gelatine and the vanilla. Beat the whites of the eggs to a stiff froth, strain the custard into them, and then stir all together. Pour into small molds and set away to serve cold.

Quantity:

This will serve six persons.

SPANISH CREAM.

Materials:

⅓ box gelatine, or 1½ tablespoonfuls of granulated gelatine.	1 pint milk.
	3 eggs.
	4 tablespoonfuls sugar.
4 tablespoonfuls cold water.	1 tablespoonful vanilla.

Way of Preparing:

Soak gelatine in four tablespoonfuls cold water. When dissolved put it with the milk in a double boiler. Add the sugar to the yolks of eggs and beat till very light. Turn into the hot milk and stir, as for a soft custard. Take from range, and add the well-beaten whites of eggs, and the vanilla. Turn into a mold to harden, and set in a cold place. This is best made several hours before serving. It may be varied by adding sliced peaches, oranges or strawberries, and more sugar, according to fruit.

Quantity:

Will serve six.

SUET PUDDING.

Materials:

1 cup suet.	1 cup molasses.
1 cup sour milk.	3 cups flour.
2 eggs.	½ cup sugar.
1 teaspoonful soda.	1 teaspoonful ginger.
½ teaspoonful salt.	½ teaspoonful cloves.
½ teaspoonful grated nutmeg.	½ teaspoonful cinnamon.

Way of Preparing:

Beat the eggs and add the sugar, then the suet, chopped very fine, then the molasses, and after it the flour. Dissolve the soda in the sour milk and add it to the mixture, lastly add the spices.

Pour into a buttered mold and steam three hours.

Quantity:

This will make one large or two small puddings.

The color of flour compared in sample batches of wet gluten

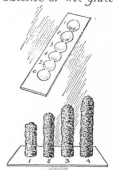

Gluten after being expanded, showing the relative strengths of the flour

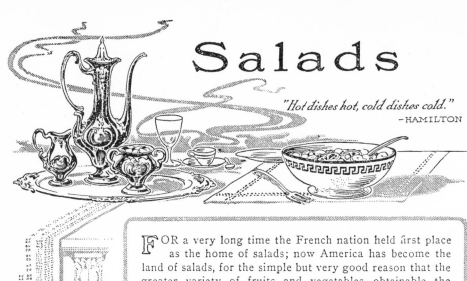

Salads

"Hot dishes hot, cold dishes cold."
—HAMILTON

FOR a very long time the French nation held first place as the home of salads; now America has become the land of salads, for the simple but very good reason that the greater variety of fruits and vegetables obtainable the year round enables us to assume the position once held by France.

As a nation we eat too few green salads and too many sweet ones. We should cultivate a taste for wholesome green foods. No absolute rules can be laid down for the making of salads, but as the simpler ones are always acceptable, begin with them and you will gradually become an expert salad-maker. The one rule applying to all salads is to have them very cold and to serve them daintily. A few of those liked most will be found herein. You can invent many others, for salads are nowadays made of everything imaginable.

AMBROSIA SALAD.

Materials:

1 pineapple.	1 quart grated cocoanut.
1 pint strawberries.	6 oranges.
4 bananas.	Sugar.
1 cup sherry wine.	

Way of Preparing:

Peel and slice the pineapple and cut the slices into thin strips. Hull the berries and cut in halves. Peel the oranges and divide into their natural divisions. Cut these in halves, sprinkle all these ingredients with sugar and put them on ice.

When ready to serve, sprinkle the bottom of a deep salad bowl with the grated cocoanut, then put in the pineapple and again some cocoanut, after that the strawberries, oranges and bananas, putting a layer of cocoanut between each two layers of fruit with a layer of cocoanut on top.

Pour over all the sherry, combined with the juices that have drained from the different fruits.

Garnish with whole strawberries, and thin slices of orange, reserved from the original materials and serve in punch cups.

Have it very cold.

Quantity:

This will serve ten persons.

CHERRY SALAD

Materials:

1 lb. large California cherries.	1 head lettuce.
½ lb. shelled hazel nuts.	10 tablespoonfuls sugar.
2 tablespoonfuls Maraschino.	½ cup sherry wine.
	2 tablespoonfuls orange juice.

Way of Preparing.

Stone the cherries and replace each stone with a blanched hazel nut. Line the salad bowl with the lettuce. Sprinkle the cherries with the sugar and pour over them a dressing made of the orange juice, sherry and maraschino.

Garnish the dish with bunches of cherries and cherry blossoms if possible.

Quantity:

This will serve six persons.

CHICKEN SALAD.

Materials:

1 chicken.	Lemon juice.
1 onion, sliced.	Celery.
1 bay leaf.	Mayonnaise.
6 cloves.	Whipped cream.
1 teaspoonful salt.	Lettuce.
½ teaspoonful white pepper.	Mace.
	Capers.

Way of Preparing:

Clean and dress the chicken. Place in boiling water, add the onion, bay leaf, cloves and mace. Bring to a boil and let it boil rapidly for five minutes. Reduce the heat to below the boiling point, and let it cook until tender.

By cooking it in this manner the dark meat will be almost as white as the meat of the breast. When the chicken is cold, cut into half-inch cubes, removing all the fat and skin. To each pint allow one tablespoonful lemon juice, sprinkle the latter over the prepared chicken and place on ice. When ready to serve, mix the chicken with two-thirds as much white celery cut into corresponding pieces. Dust with salt and pepper, mix the mayonnaise—recipe elsewhere herein—with whipped cream to taste, and pour over the salad. Serve on lettuce leaves and garnish the dish with the white leaves of the celery. Then sprinkle the top of the salad with capers.

Duck, turkey or sweetbreads may be substituted for the chicken and give you Duck Salad, Turkey Salad and Sweet Bread Salad.

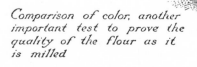

Comparison of color, another important test to prove the quality of the flour as it is milled

BOILED SALAD DRESSING.

Materials:

3 tablespoonfuls butter.
6 tablespoonfuls vinegar.
3 eggs.
6 tablespoonfuls milk.
½ teaspoonful salt.
1 teaspoonful mixed mustard.
½ teaspoonful celery salt.
¼ teaspoonful pepper.

Way of Preparing:

Put vinegar and butter into porcelain or granite pan, and place on the range. When butter is melted, take off and cool. Beat the eggs until light, add the mustard, salt, celery salt, pepper and milk. Pour this into the cooled mixture, set on range, stirring constantly from the bottom of the pan. When it begins to thicken, take off at once, and stir until smooth.

COOKED SALAD DRESSING.

Materials:

Yolks of 7 eggs.
1 cup hot vinegar.
2 cups sweet milk.
2 tablespoonfuls flour.
2 tablespoonfuls sugar.
1 teaspoonful salt.
1 teaspoonful mustard.
½ teaspoonful white pepper.
1 tablespoonful butter.

Way of Preparing:

Beat the yolks and add the sugar, salt, mustard, pepper and flour. Mix well and then add the milk slowly. Then add the hot vinegar. Cook in a double boiler until as thick as very thick cream. Remove from the fire and add the butter. Stir until the butter is all melted and thoroughly mixed.

If a milder dressing is desired add half a cup of thick cream to this mixture.

Quantity:

This will make one quart of dressing and you may bottle it while hot and keep until needed.

CUPID SALAD.

Materials:

4 oranges.
2 bananas.
⅓ cup sugar.
1 pint strawberries.
1 large tart apple.
1 egg.
1 tablespoonful brandy.

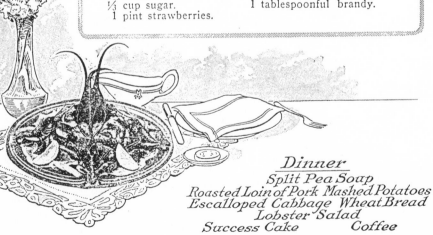

Dinner

Split Pea Soup
Roasted Loin of Pork Mashed Potatoes
Escalloped Cabbage Wheat Bread
Lobster Salad
Success Cake   Coffee

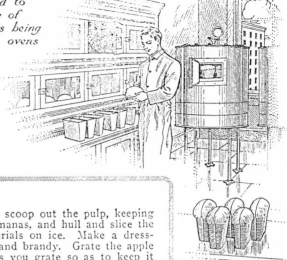

Electric sponge cabinet used to control uniform temperature of the dough preparatory to its being baked into loaves in electric ovens

Fresh loaves cut and ready for comparison

Way of Preparing:

Cut the oranges in halves, scoop out the pulp, keeping the peel intact. Slice the bananas, and hull and slice the strawberries. Place all materials on ice. Make a dressing of the apple, egg, sugar and brandy. Grate the apple and sprinkle it with sugar as you grate so as to keep it from turning dark, add to it the brandy and unbeaten white of the egg, and with a wire egg-beater beat until it is stiff and fluffy. Take the orange cups and with a pair of sharp scissors cut small scallops near the top and tie them together in pairs, using baby ribbon for tying.

When ready to serve fill the orange cups with the prepared fruit, and heap the dressing on top.

Top off each half orange with a large strawberry.

This is a pretty and significant salad to serve at a luncheon, where there are several young couples.

Place a pair of the cups on a salad plate on the table between each couple.

They can untie them or not, as they please.

Quantity:

This will serve four couples.

ENGLISH WALNUT SALAD.

Materials:

1 pint walnuts.
1 cup minced celery.
Lemon juice.
1 cup chopped apple.

1 tablespoonful olive oil.
Mayonnaise.
Lettuce.

Way of Preparing:

Soak the walnuts in lemon juice for one hour, drain, break into pieces and mix with the celery and apple. Pour over all the olive oil and place on ice for two hours. When ready to serve, place in a salad bowl lined with lettuce leaves and dress with mayonnaise. Garnish with the white leaves of the celery.

FRENCH SALAD DRESSING.

Materials:

3 tablespoonfuls olive oil.
½ teaspoonful onion juice.

1 tablespoonful vinegar.
½ teaspoonful salt.
¼ teaspoonful pepper.

Way of Preparing:

Add the salt, pepper and onion juice to the vinegar. Mix with the oil quickly and pour over the salad.

This is the most popular of all salad dressing.

English Salad Dressing

Is made by the addition of a teaspoonful of made mustard to the given quantity of French Salad Dressing.

FRUIT SALAD.

Materials:

2 doz. English walnuts.	1 cup sugar.
2 doz. white grapes.	2 tablespoonfuls lemon juice.
2 large oranges.	½ cup orange juice.
1 pineapple.	Maraschino cherries.
3 bananas.	
½ cup Madeira wine.	

Way of Preparing:

Blanch the walnut meats and break them into pieces. Skin and seed the grapes. Cut the pineapple after peeling it, into half inch cubes. Peel and slice the bananas. Peel the oranges, separate the sections, and remove the skin.

Arrange prettily on a salad dish and pour over it a dressing of—

½ cup Madeira wine.	1 cup of sugar.
2 tablespoonfuls lemon juice.	½ cup of orange juice well combined.

Garnish the whole with maraschino cherries.

Quantity:

This will serve six persons.

MACARONI AND CELERY SALAD.

Materials:

1 pint boiled macaroni.	½ pint salad dressing.
1 pint celery.	6 lettuce leaves.
½ pint chopped nuts.	

Way of Preparing:

Cut the macaroni into one half inch pieces. Cut the celery in the same manner and then mix the two.

Then add the salad dressing and sprinkle in the nuts. Line the salad dish with the lettuce leaves. Place the salad on the lettuce in the dish. Chill and serve.

Quantity:

This will serve eight persons.

MAYONNAISE.

Materials:

2 raw egg yolks.	Yolks of 2 boiled eggs.
½ pint olive oil.	2 teaspoonfuls salt.
1 teaspoonful made mus-tard.	½ teaspoonful pepper.
1 teaspoonful lemon juice.	2 tablespoonfuls vinegar.
	Sugar.

Way of Preparing:

Place your mixing bowl in a larger one full of cracked ice. Place the yolk of both raw and boiled eggs in the bowl. Drop in a little oil and rub to a cream. Add the mustard, salt, pepper and a pinch of sugar. Now add the oil, drop by drop, beating all the time until the mixture is thick and stiff enough to keep its shape and has a shiny appearance. Now thin it by addition of the vinegar, a drop at a time, until the dressing is of the proper consistency. Then add the lemon juice, and just before using add the stiffly beaten whites of the eggs.

Keep this dressing very cold.

If a mild dressing is wanted, omit the mustard and pepper. For a fruit salad omit the mustard and use the sugar instead.

For a still milder dressing omit mustard and pepper, use only half the oil, and use cream instead of the omitted oil.

PINEAPPLE SALAD.

Materials:

1 pineapple.	½ cup sherry wine.
1 pint strawberries.	½ cup orange juice.
2 oranges.	Parsley.
1 cup sugar.	

Way of Preparing:

Select a large pineapple with a straight, nice, green top. Strip off all the leaves, leaving the bud in the center. Reserve twelve of the nicest leaves. With a sharp knife cut off the top of the pineapple two inches down, leaving the center bud intact. Then take a fork and pick out all the pulps, leaving the outer wall intact. When finished you have made a nice pineapple bowl. Place this on ice. Hull the strawberries and cut in halves, reserving eighteen of the largest and nicest. Peel the oranges and cut into one-half inch cubes.

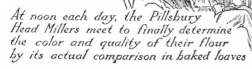

At noon each day, the Pillsbury Head Millers meet to finally determine the color and quality of their flour by its actual comparison in baked loaves

Pick the pineapple pulp into shreds and sprinkle with sugar. Place all the materials on ice for some time before serving.

When ready to serve place the twelve pineapple-top leaves in an even circle on a flat round platter, points outward. Set the pineapple bowl in the center. Fill it with alternate layers of pineapple, orange and strawberries. Mix the sherry, orange juice and half the sugar and pour over the fruit in the bowl.

Place a row of halved strawberries, flat side down, around the edge of the top of the pineapple bowl and then put on the top of the pineapple. Make a wreath around the bottom with the reserved eighteen strawberries and the parsley.

Quantity:

This will serve six persons.

POTATO SALAD.

Materials:

6 boiled potatoes, sliced while hot and allowed to cool.	2 tablespoonfuls minced celery.
1 small onion, minced fine.	1 tablespoonful minced parsley.
½ teaspoonful salt.	Boiled dressing.
	¼ teaspoonful pepper.
	Hard boiled eggs.

For the dressing use the following—

Materials:

1 cup vinegar.	1 teaspoonful salt.
2 teaspoonfuls sugar.	¼ teaspoonful pepper.
1 teaspoonful mustard.	1 cup sweet milk.
5 tablespoonfuls butter.	2 eggs.

Way of Preparing Dressing and Salad:

Melt the butter, add the salt, sugar, mustard and pepper, then add the vinegar and bring to a boil. Then stir in the milk. Stir constantly until thick. Remove from the fire and fold in the two well-beaten eggs. When ready to serve, line the salad bowl with lettuce, put in a layer of the potatoes and sprinkle with the chopped onion, celery and parsley. Alternate in this manner until all the materials are used with a layer of dressing on top.

Garnish with hard-boiled eggs in quarters, and the white leaves of the celery.

The plain French dressing may be used with the salad.

Luncheon
Beef Bouillon
Cold Tongue   Potato Salad
Raised Biscuits
Maple Perfect   Coffee

The PILLSBURY "A" Mill – the largest single Flour Mill in the World (Daily Capacity 15000 Barrels) and its Mammoth tile elevator

PILLSBURY
A
MILL
ELEVATOR

Outlet from the great twin turbines 42 ft. below the top level of St. Anthony Falls

Sandwiches

*"Variety great, to the
ingenious maker"*

SANDWICHES as a distinct dish are specifically
English and American.

They are used particularly for cold repasts, cold
lunches, and especially for outdoor refreshments at summer picnics and excursions.

Sandwiches are easily made and require for their perfection only daintiness.

Their variety is great, and largely depends upon the
ingenuity of the maker.

Chicken Salad Sandwiches.

Between two thin, oblong slices of bread, buttered, place
a layer of chicken salad on a lettuce leaf.

In making chicken salad for sandwiches, chop the
chicken and celery much finer than for ordinary purposes.

Club-House Sandwich.

Butter hot toast well; arrange half the slices on a large
platter; lay a lettuce leaf on each slice, and brush lightly
with a French dressing seasoned with mustard; then cover
with pieces of two or three kinds of meat—cold breast
of turkey sliced and a piece of freshly fried bacon, or cold
sliced tongue and fresh fried ham. Add a slice of cucumber or green tomato pickle; cover with the remaining
slices of toast and garnish with lettuce and olives. Keep
as warm as possible. Fine for luncheons.

Egg Sandwiches.

Slice hard boiled eggs or chop them fine; season with a
peanut-butter salad dressing; spread on lettuce leaves and
lay between slices of buttered bread.

Lobster Sandwiches.

Chop the lobster meat fine; season with salad dressing
to which a teaspoonful of Worcestershire sauce has been
added.

Fig Sandwich.

Thin slices of bread, cut in fancy shapes, and buttered,
with fig-filling between each two.

The fig-filling should be prepared as follows:

One-half a pound finely chopped figs, one-third cup of
sugar, half a cup of boiling water, and two tablespoonfuls
of lemon juice. Mix these ingredients and cook in a
double boiler until thick enough to spread.

Cheese Sandwiches.

Grate any good cheese, rub into a paste with butter; season with salt and a little Worcestershire sauce, and spread the bread.

Lettuce Sandwiches.

Thin, oblong slices of buttered bread, with a filling of lettuce leaves, dipped in mayonnaise and sprinkled with parmesan cheese.

Nut-Ginger Sandwiches.

Take three long, thin slices of bread, buttered. Between the first and second place a layer of chopped, preserved ginger, mixed with cream and between the second and third slices place a layer of chopped English walnuts, then tie up each sandwich neatly with baby ribbon.

Nut Sandwiches.

Thin slices of whole-wheat bread, cut circular, and buttered. The filling should be made of chopped, roasted and salted peanuts, mixed with sufficient mayonnaise to spread easily.

Peanut Sandwiches.

Grind the nuts in an Enterprise chopper and mix with sour cream salad dressing and spread thin slices of delicately buttered white bread.

Peanut Butter Sandwiches.

Mix the amount of peanut butter required with an equal amount of water, stirring them until they are thoroughly incorporated; season with salt, pepper and lemon juice to taste, and spread thin slices of bread with the mixture; lay a lettuce leaf in each sandwich and cut into any desired shape.

Ribbon Sandwiches.

Take three square, thin slices of white bread and two corresponding slices of whole wheat. Butter them and place between each two slices, the white bread being on the outside, a filling made of egg paste. Take a sharp knife and cut crosswise into thin slices, each five (three white, two whole wheat) slices of bread cut into six sandwiches.

Egg paste is prepared by mashing the yolks of three hard boiled eggs to a paste and adding two tablespoonfuls of salad dressing and pepper and salt to taste.

Luncheon
Cream of Asparagus Soup
Nut Sandwiches
Cocoa

ELABORATE French Sauces are of exquisite flavor but mysterious and difficult to make, and they are rarely attempted in the average household.

With the following simple recipes, however, with good materials and careful, unhurried attention, all will succeed.

These delicate, velvety sauces will go far toward making any meal enjoyable

BROWN SAUCE.

Materials:

1 heaping tablespoonful butter.	1 tablespoonful flour.
	1 cup boiling water.
1 tablespoonful chopped onion.	1 teaspoonful beef extract.
	1 tablespoonful tomato catsup.
1 tablespoonful chopped carrot.	1 teaspoonful caramel coloring.
1 tablespoonful chopped parsley.	

Way of Preparing:

Melt your butter in a frying pan, add the chopped vegetables and cook ten minutes, taking care not to burn the butter. Then add the flour and stir until it is a light brown. Gradually add the boiling water, beef extract, salt, tomato catsup, and lastly the coloring. Cook five minutes and strain. It is then ready for use.

Two tablespoonfuls of chopped mushrooms can be added if

Mushroom Sauce

is wanted.

CARAMEL COLORING.

Materials:

1 pint sugar.   1 pint cold water.

Way of Preparing:

Melt the sugar in a saucepan over a brisk fire. Cook until it is a dark brown, and almost burned. It will be hard and brittle and bitter to the taste. Now add slowly the cold water, stirring all the time. Boil until it is as thick as molasses. If too thick add water and boil again. Put in bottles. Keep corked and it will never spoil.

This is used for coloring soups, sauces, gravies, and in cake making.

Dinner
Mulligatawny Soup
Chicken   Sweet Potatoes
Tennessee Corn   White Bread
Frozen Pudding   Coffee

Breakfast
Fruit
Bacon   Creamed Potatoes
Muffins   Coffee

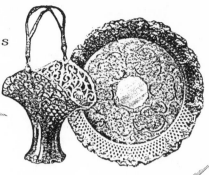

HORSE RADISH SAUCE.

Materials:

1 cup cream, scalded.   ½ teaspoonful salt.
2 tablespoonfuls freshly
   grated horseradish.

Way of Preparing:

Place the cream in a double boiler and bring to the boiling point, add the horseradish, cook two minutes and remove from the fire, then add the salt and serve.

LEMON SAUCE.

Materials:

1 cup sugar.   1½ cups boiling water.
1 tablespoonful flour.   ½ lemon, sliced.
1 heaping tablespoonful   Pinch salt.
   butter.

Way of Preparing:

Mix the sugar and flour, add the boiling water, put on the fire and when it begins to boil add the butter, sliced lemon and salt. Cook until it has the consistency of cream. Remove from the fire and serve either hot or cold.

Orange Sauce

is made by substituting one orange for the lemon, and

Chocolate Sauce

by adding two squares of Baker's unsweetened chocolate to the orange sauce.

MINT SAUCE.

Materials:

2 doz. (one bunch)   2 tablespoonfuls sugar.
   sprigs of mint.   Juice of one lemon.
½ cup of boiling water.   ½ teaspoonful salt.

Way of Preparing:

Chop the mint leaves very fine, and pour over them the boiling water, let stand for half an hour, then add the lemon juice, the salt and sugar.

TARTARE SAUCE

is one cup of mayonnaise with the addition of one tablespoonful of chopped capers, olives or pickles, and one teaspoonful of onion juice.

Dinner
Oxtail Soup
Hamburger Steak   Hashed Sweet Potatoes
Corn Bread   Potatoes
Cabbage Salad   Apple Dumplings
Coffee

TOMATO SAUCE.

Materials:

1 can tomatoes.	2 tablespoonfuls butter.
1 stalk celery.	2 tablespoonfuls flour.
1 small onion, sliced.	1 teaspoonful beef extract.
2 sprigs parsley.	Salt and pepper.
1 bay leaf.	

Way of Preparing:

Cook the tomatoes, celery, onion, parsley and bay leaf twenty-five minutes, strain and return to the double boiler. Cream butter and flour together, and add them to the previous mixture, then add the beef extract and salt and pepper to taste. It is then ready to serve.

If thicker than desired, thin with boiling water.

WHITE SAUCE.

Materials:

1 cup of milk.	2 tablespoonfuls butter.
1 tablespoonful flour.	½ teaspoonful salt.
¼ teaspoonful white pepper.	½ teaspoonful onion juice.

Way of Preparing:

Heat the milk in a double boiler, cream butter and flour together and add them to the milk. Cook until it has the consistency of cream; add the salt, pepper and onion juice, cook one minute longer and serve.

Note.—When using this sauce for sweetbreads or chicken, substitute one tablespoonful of orange juice for the onion juice. When using it for oysters, substitute two tablespoonfuls of sherry wine for the onion juice and add half a cup of thick sweet cream.

FRUIT SAUCES AND PRESERVES.

CLARIFIED APPLES.

Materials:

1 cup water.	6 large tart apples.
2 cups sugar.	½ lemon.

Way of Preparing:

Make a syrup of the sugar and water. Peel the apples, cut each in six pieces and cook in the hot syrup until clear. Remove from the syrup and place in a glass dish. When all the apples are cooked add the lemon rind and juice to the syrup. Boil it until thick, remove the lemon rind and pour over the apples.

In peeling the apples, peel and cook but two at a time if you wish them to be a very light yellow in color. If the apples are crowded in the kettle you cannot handle them easily, and if allowed to stand after peeling, they will turn dark.

Quantity:

This will serve six.

CRANBERRY SAUCE.

In making cranberry sauce do not use any water in the cooking. Wash and pick the berries and put them in a double boiler to cook. Stir them when they begin to soften, and when they are reduced to an even pulp remove them from the fire and pass them through a colander. Return to the fire and sweeten to taste.

Cook long enough to melt and combine the sugar. This makes a stiff jelly. If you wish it thinner add a little water when cooking the second time.

RHUBARB SAUCE.

Should be made in the same manner as cranberry sauce.

GINGER PEARS.

Materials:

1 quart preserved ginger.   6 lbs. sugar.
Juice of five lemons.   2 oranges.
Rind of five lemons.   Hot water.
8 lbs. pears.

Way of Preparing:

Cut the ginger in thin slices. Press out the juice of the five lemons and the oranges and cut their rind into shreds. Peel the pears and cut them crosswise in the slices. Add enough hot water to the sugar to dissolve the latter. When hot add the lemon juice, orange juice, ginger, lemon rind and orange peel. Lastly add the pears and cook slowly three hours. Place in pint fruit jars and seal. Keep in cool, dry place.

Never tiring, ever accurate machines on the packing floor, automatically fill, weigh, seal and chute into waiting cars an endless stream of barrels and sacks.

$\mathcal{S}$OUPS are of two classes: soups made with "stock" and soups without.

To the former class belong bouillon, brown stock, white stock, consommé and lambstock or mutton broth.

Soups without stock are classed as cream soups, purées and bisques.

Soups often take their names from the different nations using them.

BOUILLON.

Materials:

3 lbs. lean beef.	1 tablespoonful salt.
2 lbs. lean veal.	⅓ cup potatoes.
1 lb. marrowbone.	⅓ cup celery.
6 cups cold water.	⅓ cup onion.
10 pepper corns.	⅓ cup turnip, finely chopped.

Way of Preparing:

Put the meat and marrow bone into the soup kettle. Put in the water and let it stand covered one hour. Heat slowly to the boiling point. Remove the scum and cook for four hours. Add the vegetables and seasoning and cook two hours. Strain and allow it to get cold. Remove the fat when it is cold. Serve in cups.

Quantity:

This will serve six people.

ICED BOUILLON.

This is plain bouillon with the addition of Madeira wine or sherry, according to taste. Have it very cold when serving.

CREAM OF CELERY SOUP.

Materials:

2 cups white stock.	3 tablespoonfuls flour.
2 cups celery (cut in inch pieces).	1 pint milk.
	½ pint cream.
2 cups hot water.	1 teaspoonful salt.
1 small onion.	½ teaspoonful white pepper.
3 tablespoonfuls butter.	

Way of Preparing:

Parboil celery in water for fifteen minutes, drain and add the celery to the stock. Cook until the celery is very soft. Rub it through a sieve. Scald the onion in the milk.

Luncheon
Cream of Tomato Soup
Egg Croquettes Delicate Corn Bread
Stuffed Dates Cereal Coffee

Remove the onion and add the milk to t e stock. Cream the flour and butter together and add them also to the stock. Lastly add the cream and season with the salt and pepper.

Quantity:

The above will serve six persons.

Note.—Other cream soups are made in the same manner by using the particular vegetable instead of celery.

CREAM OF TOMATO SOUP.

Materials:

½ can tomatoes.	2 tablespoonfuls flour.
1 quart sweet milk.	3 tablespoonfuls butter.
1 tablespoonful sugar.	1 teaspoonful salt.
1 small onion.	¼ teaspoonful pepper.
1 pinch of soda.	½ cup cold water.

Way of Preparing:

Scald the milk with the onion. Remove the onion and add the flour mixed with the water, taking care to keep the mixture free from lumps. Cook the tomatoes fifteen minutes. Add the sugar and soda and pass through a sieve. Combine the mixtures and add the butter and seasoning.

Strain into a tureen and serve at once.

Quantity:

The above soup will serve six persons.

OXTAIL SOUP.

Materials:

1 oxtail cut in small pieces.	1 teaspoonful salt.
5 cups brown stock.	¼ teaspoonful pepper.
Carrot cut in dice.	½ cup Madeira wine.
Celery cut in dice.	1 teaspoonful Worcestershire sauce.
Onion cut in dice.	Juice of half a lemon.
Turnip cut in dice.	Butter.

Way of Preparing:

Dredge the oxtail in flour and fry in butter until nicely browned. Add it to the stock and simmer two hours. Parboil the vegetables ten minutes, drain them and add them to the stock. Cook until the vegetables are tender, then add salt, pepper, wine, sauce and lemon juice. Let it cook ten minutes and serve.

Quantity:

This will serve six persons.

MULLIGATAWNY SOUP.

Materials:

5 cups white stock.	2 tablespoonfuls butter.
1 pint raw chicken, (cut in dice.)	3 tablespoonfuls flour.
1 cup tomatoes.	2 sprigs parsley.
½ cup of onion.	3 cloves.
½ cup of celery.	1 blade mace.
½ cup of carrot.	1 apple, sliced.
1 pepper, chopped.	1 teaspoonful curry powder.
	Salt and pepper.

Way of Preparing:

Cook the vegetables and chicken in butter until brown. Add the flour, mace, curry powder, cloves, parsley, tomatoes and stock and simmer one hour. Strain, reserving the chicken and rub the vegetables through a sieve, add the chicken to the soup, season with salt and pepper (according to taste) and serve with boiled rice.

The apple is included in the vegetables.

Quantity:

This will serve eight persons.

POTATO SOUP.

Materials:

3 potatoes.	1 teaspoonful salt.
1 quart milk.	¼ teaspoonful pepper.
1 onion.	2 tablespoonfuls butter.
2 stalks celery.	1 tablespoonful flour.

Way of Preparing:

Cook the potatoes in salted water with the onion. When soft, mash the potatoes smooth and rub through a fine sieve. Scald the milk with the celery. Remove the celery and add the butter and flour creamed together. Then add the prepared potatoes to the milk and season with the salt and pepper. Let it come to a boil and serve at once.

Quantity:

This soup will serve six persons.

SPLIT PEA SOUP.

Materials:

1 cup dried split peas.	1 teaspoonful salt.
2 quarts cold water.	¼ teaspoonful white pepper.
1 pint milk.	
1 small onion.	2-inch cube salt pork.
2 tablespoonfuls butter.	2 tablespoonfuls flour.

Way of Preparing:

Soak the peas over night, drain and add the water, pork and onion sliced. Simmer until the peas are very soft, and then rub them through a sieve. Cream the butter and flour together and add to the peas. Then add salt, pepper and milk.

Reheat and serve hot.

Quantity:

This will serve six persons.

BROWN STOCK.

Materials:

5 lbs. shin beef.	⅓ cup potato.
½ gallon water.	⅓ cup turnip.
10 pepper corns.	⅓ cup onion.
5 cloves.	⅓ cup carrot.
1 bay leaf.	⅓ cup celery, coarsely chop-
1 tablespoonful salt.	ped.
2 sprigs parsley.	

Way of Preparing:

Cut the lean meat in inch pieces and brown it in a hot frying pan, using the marrow from the bone. Put the bone and fat in the kettle. Add the cold water and let it stand for twenty minutes. Put it over the fire and bring it to the boiling point. Remove the scum as it rises and add the browned meat. Cover the kettle. Reduce heat and cook the meat at the boiling point for five hours. Add the prepared vegetables and seasoning and cook for two hours. Strain and cool immediately.

WHITE STOCK.

Materials:

4 lbs. knuckle of veal.	1 small onion.
1 lb. lean beef.	2 stalks celery.
2½ quarts cold water.	1 bayleaf.
10 pepper corns.	1 tablespoonful salt.

Way of Preparing:

Remove the meat from the bone and cut it in small pieces. Do the same with the beef, only make the pieces smaller. Put meat and bone into a kettle and add the water. Bring it slowly to a boil and skim carefully. Simmer for five hours. Strain twice through several thicknesses of cheesecloth and the stock will be clear. White stock can be made from the water in which a fowl or chicken is cooked.

Quantity:

The above recipe will produce three pints of soup-stock.

A single carload of "Pillsbury's Best" flour will make almost a 100,000 loaves of bread

Vegetables

$\mathbb{V}$EGETABLES should first of all be fresh, or at least perfectly fresh.

In planning meals, consider the appropriate place for certain vegetables with different meats. Vegetables and the mode of preparing them should be varied from day to day, but any fresh, green vegetable served very cold, or any well-cooked vegetable served very hot, will always be appreciated.

Boiled vegetables should be cooked in an abundance of salted water, and served quickly, as soon as they are done.

It is considered a valuable secret by some French cooks, that green vegetables will retain their bright color if boiled in an open kettle.

BAKED BEANS.

1 pint beans.	1 teaspoon mustard.
½ lb. salt pork.	1 teaspoon sugar.
½ teaspoon molasses.	1 small onion.

Pick the beans and let them soak over night in water. In the bottom of a bean jar put half the pork and the onion, then pour in half the beans. Add the remainder of the pork and the rest of the beans, then the molasses, mustard and sugar. Cover with boiling water and bake from six to seven hours in a moderate oven, keeping them covered with water until the last hour.

Be sure and have cover on bean jar while in the oven.

CARAMELIZED SWEET POTATOES.

Materials:

1 dozen small sweet potatoes.	1 pint brown sugar.
	1 cup hot water.
2 quarts hot water.	1 tablespoonful butter.
1 teaspoonful salt.	½ teaspoonful cinnamon.

Way of Preparing:

Boil the potatoes in two quarts of hot water until they are tender. Peel and arrange in a shallow baking dish. Boil the cup of water and sugar together for ten minutes. Sprinkle salt and cinnamon over the potatoes and add the butter to the sauce. Then pour the sauce over the potatoes and bake in a moderate oven until the potatoes are nicely browned.

Serve in the dish in which they were baked.

Quantity:

This will serve six people.

DEVILED POTATOES.

Materials:

2 dozen small new potatoes.	¼ teaspoonful pepper.
	1 teaspoonful salt.
1 teaspoonful mustard.	2 tablespoonfuls vinegar.
2 heaping tablespoonfuls butter.	1 cup lard.
	2 egg yolks.

Way of Preparing:

Boil the potatoes until nearly done. Peel them, heat the lard in a frying pan and fry the potatoes until they are a nice golden-brown color. Melt the butter in a saucepan and add the pepper, salt, mustard and vinegar. Now place the potatoes in the saucepan and let them simmer three minutes. Remove to a hot dish. Add the eggs to the sauce. Pour it over the potatoes and serve.

Quantity:

Two dozen potatoes to serve six.

EGG PLANT.

Materials:

1 large egg plant.	2 eggs.
1 quart boiling water.	½ cup flour.
1 tablespoonful salt.	Deep fat.
1 cup cracker crumbs.	

Way of Preparing:

Cut your egg plant into one-half inch slices. Remove the peel. Pour over it the quart of boiling water after dissolving in it the salt. Let it stand one hour, drain off the water, wipe the slices dry, flour lightly, dip in beaten egg, and then in the crumbs and fry in the deep fat. Serve very hot.

Quantity:

This will serve five persons.

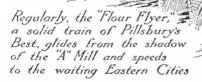

Regularly, the "Flour Flyer," a solid train of Pillsbury's Best, glides from the shadow of the "A" Mill and speeds to the waiting Eastern Cities

GREEN PEPPERS STUFFED WITH CORN.

Materials:

6 large sweet peppers.	½ cup cream.
2 cups green corn.	½ cup boiling water.
3 tablespoonfuls butter.	1 teaspoonful salt.
3 tablespoonfuls boiling water.	½ teaspoonful pepper.

Way of Preparing:

With a sharp knife cut around three-fourths of the stem end of each pepper, leaving it hinged by the other fourth as a lid. Remove the seeds and inner membranes. Cover the pepper with cold water, and bring it to a boil. Drain off the water, cover them with fresh boiling water and simmer until tender. Drain, sprinkle lightly with salt, and allow to cool. Put two tablespoonfuls of butter into frying pan and heat it. When hot add the green corn and the three tablespoonfuls of hot water. Cook five minutes and add the cream and seasonings. Now cook slowly until quite thick. Let the mixture then cool and fill your prepared peppers with it. Fasten down the stem-end lids of the peppers and place them in a buttered baking dish. Melt the remaining tablespoonful of butter in the half cup of boiling water, pour the liquid over the peppers and bake for twenty-five minutes. These will be found delicious to serve with fish courses.

Quantity:

This will serve six people.

HASHED BROWN POTATOES WITH GRAVY.

Materials:

3 cups cold, boiled potatoes, sliced.	1 teaspoonful salt.
1 onion.	½ teaspoonful pepper.
1 tablespoonful flour.	½ bay leaf.
1 cup boiling water.	1 tablespoonful tomato catsup.
3 tablespoonfuls butter.	

Way of Preparing:

Melt one tablespoonful of butter in a saucepan, add the flour and brown carefully; then add a cup of boiling water, leaving out three tablespoonfuls of it. Now add the salt, pepper, one-half the onion (sliced thin), and the half bay leaf. Melt one tablespoonful of butter in the three of boiling water and moisten your potatoes with this mixture. Rub a frying pan with the other half of the onion, place in it a tablespoonful of butter and heat very hot

Dinner
Split Pea Soup
Fried Spring Chicken
Hashed Brown Potatoes Carrots
Graham Bread
Rice Pudding Coffee

Breakfast
Boiled Rice
Boiled Tomatoes
Doughnuts
Cream Sauce
Coffee

Pour in the prepared potatoes and brown. Turn the potatoes out like an omelette onto a hot platter, strain the gravy and add the tomato catsup. Serve the strained gravy in a sauceboat with the potatoes, or pour it around them on the platter.

Quantity:

This will serve six persons.

RICE.

Wash and cleanse the rice. Then pour boiling hot water on it—half a gallon of water to one cup of raw rice —and let it boil without stirring. it for from twenty-five to thirty minutes, according to the quality of your rice. When the kernels, although each seems separate and independent, are soft, pour off the water, return it to the fire and let it steam until it seems dry. Then your rice is done and you may serve it either with brown butter, or with sugar and cream, or with sugar and powdered cinnamon mixed, or with the juice or gravy of any roast.

SCALLOPED CABBAGE.

Materials:

1 quart cabbage, prepared as for slaw.	1 tablespoonful flour.
1 teaspoonful salt.	1 teaspoonful salt.
1 quart boiling water.	½ teaspoonful pepper.
1 cup sweet milk.	1 cup fine cracker crumbs.
2 tablespoonfuls butter.	1 tablespoonful butter.

Way of Preparing:

Pour the boiling water on the cabbage and add one teaspoonful of salt. Boil fifteen minutes. Drain off the water. Heat the milk, cream the two tablespoonfuls of butter and the flour and add them to the milk. Then add one teaspoonful of salt and the pepper. Cook to the consistency of thick cream. Remove from the fire. Butter a small pudding dish and sprinkle the bottom with cracker crumbs. Put in half your cabbage, then half the sauce, sprinkle with cracker crumbs, then add the remaining cabbage, then the sauce and cover thickly with cracker crumbs. Dot it with small pieces of butter, cover and bake in a moderate oven twenty-five minutes, uncover and brown. Serve from the dish in which it was baked.

Quantity:

This will serve six persons.

115

Luncheon
Cold Roast Beef
Stuffed Onions
Whole Wheat Gems
Fruit Salad   Plain Cake
Coffee

STUFFED ONIONS.

Materials:

6 large onions.
1 cup finely chopped raw beef.
1 cup soft bread crumbs.
1 teaspoonful salt.
½ teaspoonful pepper.

1 egg.
¼ cup cream.
1 tablespoonful melted butter.
½ cup cracker crumbs.
1 tablespoonful boiling water.

Way of Preparing:

Peel and parboil the onions in salted water ten minutes, remove and drain. When cooled remove the center of each onion. Add the cream and well-beaten egg to the boiling water. To this add the bread crumbs and the chopped beef, together with the seasonings and fill the centers of the onions with this mixture. Brush the top of the onions with melted butter, sprinkle with cracker crumbs, place in a shallow, buttered baking dish, cover it and bake until onions are tender, then uncover and continue baking until they are brown.

Quantity:

This will serve six persons.

STUFFED TOMATOES.

Materials:

8 medium-sized firm tomatoes.
1 cup cold chicken, chopped fine.
1 tablespoonful salt.
1 cup cracker crumbs.

1 teaspoonful onion juice.
1 cup of soup stock.
1 egg.
2 tablespoonfuls cream.
1 pinch pepper.
Toast.

Way of Preparing:

Cut a small slice from the top of each tomato, and scoop out the pulp with a spoon. Sprinkle the tomatoes on the inside with salt. Turn them upside down on a platter and let them stand half an hour. Remove the seeds from the pulps, drain off the juice and make a stuffing, using the chopped chicken, tomato pulp, cracker crumbs, egg, cream, onion juice, pepper and a teaspoonful of salt. Wipe the tomatoes dry inside and out and fill each with the prepared stuffing. Place in a baking dish, pour the soup stock around them and bake in a moderately hot oven until the tomatoes are tender, but not falling to pieces. You should baste the tomatoes frequently with the stock while baking. Serve immediately, placing each tomato on a square of toast.

Quantity:

This will serve eight people.

SPAGHETTI A L'ITALIENNE.

Materials:

1 cupful of hot water.	2 tablespoons butter.
1 can tomatoes.	2 tablespoonsful flour.
1 tablespoonful sugar.	8 peppercorns.
2 heaping tablespoonsful onion (cut fine).	1 teaspoonful salt. Bit of bay leaf.
1 teaspoonful of Beef Extract.	1 sprig of parsley.

Way of Preparing:

Cook the tomatoes twenty minutes with the onion peppercorns, bay leaf, parsley and salt. Rub through a strainer. Add the Extract of Beef. Brown the butter and add the flour. When well blended add to the hot liquid and the sugar. Stir well; pour over spaghetti and serve with grated cheese.

The spaghetti should be cooked in long strips rather than broken into small pieces. To accomplish this hold the quantity to be cooked in the hand and dip the ends into boiling salted water. As the spaghetti softens it will bend and may be coiled under the water. Cook spaghetti thirty minutes.

TENNESSEE CORN.

Materials:

1 quart green corn.	2 tablespoonfuls melted butter.
2 eggs.	
1 teaspoonful salt.	3 tablespoonfuls cream.
½ teaspoonful pepper.	1 cup milk.

Way of Preparing:

With a sharp knife cut enough green corn from the cobs to fill a quart measure. Heat the milk. Beat the eggs and add to them the cream and seasonings, then add the butter, and scalded milk. Place the corn in a buttered pudding dish, and pour the liquid mixture over it. Bake in a slow oven until firm. Serve hot as a side dish with a meat course.

Quantity:
This will serve six persons.

SPINACH.

Pick over carefully while dry, throw a few plants at a time into a large pan of cold water, wash well on both sides to dislodge insects, and pass to another pan. They should have at least three separate waters. Put the spinach into a large kettle without water, set it on the stove where it will cook slowly till the juice is drawn, then boil till tender, drain and chop fine. For half a peck of spinach add one ounce butter, one-half teaspoon salt. Reheat and serve on buttered toast.

TABLE SERVICE.

IN household cooking, consult the tastes of the family, and adapt the menus of the different days to include the favorite dishes of each member. With or without guests, a charming hostess may observe a plain and easy style of entertaining.

The smaller the dinner, the more surety of its being well planned and served, and thoroughly successful.

The housekeeper needs not so much technical knowledge as every-day appreciation of what is good and healthful to eat.

A poor table may be wasteful.

To dine with comfort and pleasure, to promote health. and at the same time to keep the cook good natured and happy, the diner and the dinner should be ready at the same time.

The hot dishes should be hot and the cold dishes always cold. To have your coffee and salad both lukewarm is ruinous indeed.

To be original is the gift of genius, otherwise, originality would be without charm and become commonplace. It is every woman's desire to introduce something new and different from the ordinary in the way of preparing attractive dishes and providing artistic table decorations varied for different occasions. The food, service and decorations of a simple luncheon, are oftentimes remembered far more than those of the greatest banquets.

Too much attention can scarcely be paid to the looks of food that we bring to our tables and the way in which it is served.

Ice for drinking water should be carefully washed and cleaned before using. Never touch it with the hands, but place in glass with ice scoop or tongs.

In preparing fancy drinks of any kind, it is most essential to ornament them with slices of fruit in season.

The far reaches of the sea — Europe, Australia, Japan or the Philippines — all these know and eat Minnesota Flour

Supper
Potato and Cucumber Salad
Sandwiches
Tea or Coffee

TABLE SERVICE.

Formal meals are served from the table by the host or hostess, and with the assistance of attendants from pantry or separate table. But in either case, food should always be set down before the guest, from the right. Dishes from which guest is to help himself, should be presented, or passed to his left. In finishing the course, plates should also be removed from the left. The manners and care of the attendants are most important. Dishes should be removed one at a time, not stacked on the table by the guests or attendant and crowded upon a tray, but taken away and placed on a tray separately.

In setting a table for luncheon or dinner, place a plate for each person. To the left lay forks in the order of their use. First, the dinner fork to be at the extreme left. At the right, the required silver in the order of their use, beginning with an oyster fork next to the plate, followed by soup spoon, knives, etc. Tea and dessert spoons should be placed separately to the right in front of the plate. The bowl of the forks or spoon should be turned upwards, and cutting edges of the knife towards the plate. Napkins should be placed to the left of the forks. Water glasses should be placed beyond the tops of the knives, or before the plate when wine is served in its former place. Wine glasses should be placed in the order in which they are served. The first should be to the extreme right, and nearest the hand. Fish or salad forks should be placed either separately, just beyond the forks to the left, or placed among them according to their time of use with the menu, or be placed separately to the left just before either salad or dessert is served. The same is applied to either fancy or plain spoons used for dessert or after dinner coffee, but the latter (should not be) placed among knives or silverware to the right, if laid at the beginning of the meal. When salad or dessert, fork or spoon are left, same should be reset in their respective places (left or right) before serving this course.

Luncheon
Clam Chowder – Chocolate Cake
Coffee

HEALTH BRAN MUFFINS.

Materials:

2 cups Pillsbury's Health Bran.
2 cups Pillsbury's Best Flour.
1½ teaspoons salt.
2 cups sour milk or buttermilk.
½ cup sugar.
1 tablespoon lard or butter.
1 egg.
1½ teaspoons baking soda.
½ cup water.

Way of Preparing:

Beat butter, egg and sugar together until creamy. To the sour milk add the soda dissolved in the water (boiling), then the bran, flour, salt, and the egg and sugar mixture. Mix thoroughly and divide into buttered gem pans and bake in a hot oven for twenty minutes.

Muffins may be warmed over by placing in oven for a few minutes.

HEALTH BRAN BREAD.

Materials:

6 cups Pillsbury's Health Bran.
5 cups Pillsbury's Best Flour.
4 tablespoons molasses (not too dark).
2 teaspoons sugar.
2 teaspoons salt.
1 cake compressed yeast.
½ teaspoon soda.
3 cups water (lukewarm).

Way of Preparing:

Mix the flour, bran and soda thoroughly. Dissolve yeast in a half cup of the water. Add molasses, sugar and salt in the balance of the water, then add the yeast. Stir thoroughly. Then add flour, bran and soda, mixing thoroughly and adding a little more flour if necessary. Form into a ball with the hands and set to rise. If the temperature is right (80° to 82° F.) it will require 2¼ hours, then knead well and let rise for ¾ hour longer. Divide and mould into two loaves, place same in pans, let rise for ½ hour longer then bake for ¾ hour in a moderate oven— 450° F. is the proper temperature.

HEALTH BRAN COOKIES.

Materials:

3 cups Pillsbury's Health Bran.
1½ cups Pillsbury's Best Flour.
⅔ cup milk.
½ cup sugar.

½ cup butter.
2 eggs.
2 level tablespoons baking powder.
Chopped raisins if desired.

Way of Preparing:

Cream the butter and sugar together, add the well beaten eggs, then the milk gradually. Mix baking powder with flour and bran and add gradually to the above. If the dough cannot be handled add a little more flour. Roll out thin, cut with a cookie cutter and bake in a quick oven from 7 to 10 minutes.

HEALTH BRAN PANCAKES.

Materials:

2 measuring cups Health Bran.
1 measuring cup Pillsbury's Best Flour.
2 measuring cups sour milk.
1 tablespoonful of water.
1 teaspoonful of soda.
1 teaspoonful of salt.
1 (only) egg.

Way of Preparing:

Mix well and bake on a hot griddle.

Quantity:

This receipt is enough for a family of four.

Dinner

Lamb Chops   Creamed Potatoes
Baked Egg Plant
Gooseberry Custard
Coffee

WHAT IS YEAST?

YEAST is a microscopic plant of fungus growth, a col- lection of living one-celled organisms that partake of the nature of plant life.

How Does it Grow?

With proper warmth, moisture and food, the walls of these little one-celled plants bulge on the side in an oval shape. This bulge soon separates from the parent cell and becomes an independent organism. Other cells form in the same way from the parent cell, and also from each new cell, and thus the yeast plant multiplies.

What of its Care?

The little yeast cells are tenacious of life, and can live under most adverse circumstances. They are killed by exposure to heat above the boiling point of water, but they endure cold much better, being able to continue life in a suspended form at two degrees below freezing. From 65 to 72 degrees Fahrenheit is most favorable to the growth of yeast. The best collection of yeast cells massed together in a dormant state, is the ordinary yeast cake, either dry or compressed.

How Long Does it Live?

Yeast cells may be kept alive and vigorous for many days if kept in a dry and cool place.

What is its Relation to Flour and Bread?

The yeast is softened in water to separate the yeast cells that they may be easily distributed through the flour.

In the starch and gluten of the flour, they find their food. Sugar hastens their growth, while salt retards it.

The yeast cells, finding their favorite food, begin to grow, changing the starch of the flour into sugar, and the sugar into carbonic gas and alcohol. The gas, in its efforts to escape, expands the elastic gluten of the dough in which it is mixed, and lifting up the mixture, the bread is "raised."

By subjecting the dough to heat (baking), the alcohol and carbonic gas are driven out and the cell-walls are fixed, and thus sweet bread is produced.

For reasons stated above, your flour and utensils should always be warm.

The life of the yeast is constantly in jeopardy, while age to flour, if properly kept in dry place, improves its quality.

INDEX

PILLSBURY FLOUR MILLS CO.

DEPARTMENT "A"

MINNEAPOLIS   -   MINNESOTA

Find enclosed ten cents for which send
"The Pillsbury Cook Book" to

Name _____

No. and Street _____

City _____ State _____

FOLD HERE

Fold this end on
dotted line and
place ten cents in
money or stamps
in it.

FOLD HERE

FOLD HERE

Cut. fold and mail with coin in sealed envelope.

A PASS

THE Minneapolis Flour Mills are the wonder of the world.   Chief among them is the famous "Pillsbury A" Mill — the largest single flouring mill in existence.

This card when presented at the "A" Mill office will permit you to visit this most interesting building.

A courteous guide will accompany you, explaining and illustrating the process of milling and the conditions of absolute purity which everywhere prevail in the manufacture of "Pillsbury's Best" flour.

Thousands of other people annually avail themselves of this highly entertaining and instructive experience. Will you not, when next in Minneapolis, give us the opportunity to take you through?

PILLSBURY FLOUR MILLS CO.
MINNEAPOLIS. MINN.

PILLSBURY FLOUR MILLS CO.

DEPARTMENT "A"

MINNEAPOLIS   -   MINNESOTA

Find enclosed ten cents for which send
"The Pillsbury Cook Book" to

Name _____

No. and Street _____

City _____ State _____

FOLD HERE

Fold this end on
dotted line and
place ten cents in
money or stamps
in it.

FOLD HERE

FOLD HERE

Cut. fold and mail with coin in sealed envelope.

This 2001 edition is published by Gramercy Books™,
an imprint of Random House Value Publishing, Inc.,
280 Park Avenue, New York, NY 10017, by arrangement with Ottenheimer Publishers,
Inc., 5 Park Center Court; Suite 300, Owings Mills, MD 21117.

Gramercy Books™ and design are trademarks of
Random House Value Publishing, Inc.

Random House
New York • Toronto • London • Sydney • Auckland
http://www.randomhouse.com/

Printed and bound in the United States of America.

A catalog record for this title is available from the Library of Congress.

ISBN 0-517-16338-1

8 7 6 5 4 3 2 1